DECODING THE IT VALUE PROBLEM

Founded in 1807, John Wiley & Sons is the oldest independent publishing company in the United States. With offices in North America, Europe, Asia, and Australia, Wiley is globally committed to developing and marketing print and electronic products and services for our customers' professional and personal knowledge and understanding.

The Wiley CIO series provides information, tools, and insights to IT executives and managers. The products in this series cover a wide range of topics that supply strategic and implementation guidance on the latest technology trends, leadership, and emerging best practices.

Titles in the Wiley CIO series include:

DECODING THE IT VALUE PROBLEM

AN EXECUTIVE GUIDE FOR ACHIEVING
OPTIMAL ROI ON CRITICAL IT INVESTMENTS

Gregory J. Fell

WILEY

Published by John Wiley & Sons, Inc., Hoboken, New Jersey.
Published simultaneously in Canada.

For general information on our other products and services or for technical support, please contact our Customer Care Department within the United States at (800) 762-2974, outside the United States at (317) 572-3993 or fax (317) 572-4002.

Wiley publishes in a variety of print and electronic formats and by print-on-demand. Some material included with standard print versions of this book may not be included in e-books or in print-on-demand. If this book refers to media such as a CD or DVD that is not included in the version you purchased, you may download this material at http://booksupport.wiley.com. For more information about Wiley products, visit www.wiley.com.

Library of Congress Cataloging-in-Publication Data:

Fell, Gregory J., 1964-
   Decoding the IT value problem, + website : an executive guide for achieving optimal ROI on critical IT investments / Gregory J. Fell.
      pages cm. — (Wiley CIO)
   ISBN 978-1-118-43805-3 (hardback); ISBN 978-1-118-75409-2 (ebk);
   ISBN 978-1-118-75433-7 (ebk)
   1. Information technology.   2. Information technology—Cost effectiveness.
   3. Capital investments—Evaluation.   I. Title.
   HD30.2.F4567 2013
004.068'1—dc23
                                                                    2013017991

Printed in the United States of America

10 9 8 7 6 5 4 3 2 1

For my Computer Club brothers, who toiled on weekends solving big-endian/little-endian problems and kernel panics. We have changed the world forever.

CONTENTS

FOREWORD: UNCOVERING AN ESSENTIAL SKILL OF IT MANAGEMENT

I have spent the past three decades providing high-level thought leadership services to the information technology (IT) industry. I have written three books about IT leadership: *The Transformational CIO, On Top of the Cloud,* and *Leading the Epic Revolution.* I also write a weekly blog and newsletter on current IT leadership topics.

As a consequence of my work, I read a lot about the role of IT in the modern business enterprise. Here is something I have noticed: Most of the books and articles about IT management tend to focus primarily on either technology (hard skills) or leadership (soft skills).

After reading a draft of Greg's manuscript, however, I realized that what's missing from many of those books is a detailed discussion of a third critical skill: business acumen.

Without business acumen, it is hard to run an IT department for any reasonable period of time. Despite its importance, the subject of business acumen rarely surfaces in conversations about IT leadership.

Greg's book remedies that situation. It is specifically written to provide sound business advice to C-level executives who are responsible for making decisions about IT investments.

If you are a CEO, CFO, or COO, this book will help you ask better and more relevant questions when the CIO proposes new IT projects. It will help you understand the IT value proposition more thoroughly and develop a deeper understanding of how IT drives growth and revenue in today's economy.

If you are a CIO, this book will serve as a practical guide for delivering consistently higher returns on IT investments and avoiding the unseen dangers that can undermine IT projects.

Greg's book covers essential topics that are often overlooked or given short shrift in discussions between the CIO and other C-level executives. Those topics include balancing risk and exposure, why IT projects often fail to deliver expected value, how companies should prepare for technology disruptors, why time is the enemy, and why a collaborative effort among senior executives is necessary for optimizing returns on critical IT investments.

Over the course of my career, I have spoken with thousands of leaders and executives who make decisions about IT spending. I can honestly say that almost all of them would benefit from reading this concise and well-written book.

Hunter Muller
CEO and President
HMG Strategy LLC

PREFACE

When I began this project several years ago, its original goal was helping CIOs explain the value of IT to their companies. But over the course of conducting interviews and collecting research, the emphasis of the book shifted. Instead of writing a book primarily for CIOs, I wrote a book for the entire C-suite. My decision to address a wider audience was based on my growing realization that most C-level executives (other than the CIO) believe that IT does not deliver sufficient value to their companies. Most of the senior executives that I spoke with expressed the opinion that IT is an underperforming asset.

The universality of their agreement on that point is alarming, and it points to a larger problem. It is not sufficient for the CIO to do a better job of explaining the value of IT to the company's C-suite. The C-suite must do a better job of understanding the value of IT to the company and appreciating how its decisions on IT spending impact the company's ability to compete effectively in a networked economy.

From my perspective as a C-level corporate officer, the IT value problem is a significant obstacle to success and prosperity. As a CIO, I see the problem as eminently solvable. This book lays the groundwork for decoding the IT value problem and offers actionable advice for increasing the returns on critical IT investments. It is written as both a practical guide and an executive roadmap. I hope that you find it useful and valuable.

ACKNOWLEDGMENTS

Thank you to my colleagues at Terex for their guidance and wisdom at the lunch table, forgoing politics and sports for discussions on IT budgets and governance models.

Thank you to all the participants in the book for sharing their insights and experience so generously: Kelly Bissell, Susan Certoma, Ross Kudwitt, Beverly Lieberman, Filippo Passerini, Mark Polansky, Vallabh Sambamurthy and Leo Sadovy.

Special thanks to Mike Barlow, whose guidance in writing my first book has been immeasurable.

A major thank you to Cathy and Bethany for their love and support.

DECODING THE IT VALUE PROBLEM

INTRODUCTION

I grew up in Michigan, in what was then considered the heartland of the automotive industry. Everything in that part of the country seemed dominated or influenced by machinery and technology.

Like many young people, I was fascinated by the dreamlike quality of technology. My career began in the automotive industry, which itself is a unique fusion of business, technology, and popular culture.

I entered the industry at a time when its decline seemed irreversible. I'm happy that the automotive sector is now recovering and has regained its competitive spirit.

These days, I collect sports cars and motorcycles. My garage looks a bit like an automotive repair shop and a spare parts depot. It brings me back to the days of my youth, when it seemed as though you could solve any problem with the right combination of knowledge and elbow grease.

I also have a small collection of Revolutionary War muskets. It's amazing to think that those smooth-bore flintlocks were once considered state of the art.

One day, not too long from now, we'll look back at our information technologies with a similar kind of amused wonderment.

But it seems unlikely that we will ever outgrow our need for technology. Technology is a tool, and our use of tools is what makes us human. Wooden clubs, stone knives, clay pots, jet planes, and iPhones— one thousand years from now, they'll all seem equally primitive.

But we're getting ahead of ourselves. Technology plays a huge role in our lives today and will likely play an even larger role in the future. That's why getting it right is important—determining the proper and effective use of technology isn't a trivial pursuit, it's a serious business.

I mentioned my interest in Revolutionary War weaponry earlier because it allows me to talk now about an early application of technology in our history as Americans. The year was 1776. Despite heavy losses during the Battle of Bunker Hill in the previous year, the British still controlled Boston.

Then something occurred that changed the balance of power and forced the British to flee. A small detail of rebels under the command of a 25-year-old bookseller named Henry Knox accomplished an "impossible" feat, hauling 60 tons of captured artillery 300 miles from Fort Ticonderoga in upstate New York to Dorchester Heights overlooking Boston.

When the British awoke to the see the cannons above them, they quickly left the city, handing General George Washington an important and largely bloodless victory.

From my perspective, it was a brilliant use of technology for a good cause. Knox and his team had to improvise at many points along the difficult journey, but they completed their project successfully and in the nick of time!

I find it inspiring to imagine the obstacles and problems that Knox had to overcome. I think that all of us who labor to complete difficult projects under tight deadlines and with limited resources can identify with Knox and his teammates. Thankfully, we don't have to drag heavy cannons across snow-covered mountains. But sometimes the challenges we face can seem as daunting. And hopefully, future generations will appreciate our efforts, as we appreciate the efforts of those who came before us.

CHAPTER 1

The Value of IT

EXECUTIVE SUMMARY

It is important to understand the difference between the perceived value and the real or expected value of IT projects. Small increases in perceived value can lead to huge increases in costs and greatly reduce the odds of a satisfactory outcome.

The 80/20 Law of IT Spending

Many years ago, Sir Arthur C. Clarke famously observed, "Any sufficiently advanced technology is indistinguishable from magic."

Sir Arthur's comment is, of course, brilliant. It should not, however, be applied to information technology (IT), and it should especially not be applied to decisions about IT spending.

Sure, it might be easier to see IT as some form of magic, but it would also be financially irresponsible. Remember, as a corporate executive, you have a fiduciary responsibility to the corporation and its owners. You have a legal, moral, and ethical responsibility to invest the corporation's money wisely.

So let's just say it out loud: IT isn't magic. IT is often complicated and difficult to understand, but it's not magic. And unlike magic, IT isn't free. In fact, IT can be extremely expensive. IT investments have consequences, and it's crucial to make the right judgments when you're spending the company's money.

That's why it's imperative to understand the *80/20 Law of IT Spending*. Let me put it another way: *Not* understanding the 80/20 law inevitably leads to a fundamental disconnect between IT and the business.

The 80/20 law arises from the difference between the perceived value and the true cost of IT investments. Basically, the value perceived by the user represents only 20 percent of the true cost. The impact of this discrepancy is significant: Every 5 percent boost in perceived value *doubles the cost of an IT project!*

Those incremental boosts in perceived value will no doubt make some individuals in the company happy. Over the long term, however, they can blow large holes in the company's budget. Understanding the 80/20 law will help you manage those risks.

The User Interface Is Not the Project

Despite its importance and its simplicity, the 80/20 law is widely ignored. That's because the 80/20 law is counterintuitive. People are accustomed to believing their eyes, and when they look at a user interface, they tend to see the user interface as "the project."

There are lots of analogies we could apply here: Don't judge a book by its cover. Beauty is only skin deep. Appearances can be deceiving.

You get the picture. The user interface is not the entire iceberg—it's only the tip!

The real costs are invariably behind the interface. Let's look at some specific instances.

For example, imagine that a unit of the company needs a new web site. When internal users look at the web site, they judge its value to them by looking at the user interface. What they do not see, however, is everything that's *behind* the interface, such as the servers, the network, the databases, the load balancers, and all the other technologies and services enabling the web site to perform its intended business function.

Now let's say that someone looks at the interface and says, "Hey, wouldn't it be cool if you could click on an image on the screen and it would spin around so you could see all 360 degrees of it? That shouldn't be too hard, right?"

Well, maybe it's hard and maybe it's not. That's not the issue. The real issue is how much extra it is going to cost and whether or not that extra cost can be justified. That one "little tweak" can have a huge impact on the project's cost. Remember, every 5 percent gain in perceived value translates to a doubling of cost. That's why it's critical to understand the 80/20 law.

Let's take another common example: server costs. You buy an application, and you need a server to run it. If the application will be used by a workgroup within a business unit, you can run it on a server that costs $20,000.

If, however, you want the application to be available to everyone in the company, you will need an enterprise-level server, a database, a cooling system, and some form of RAID (redundant array of independent disks) technology in case the hard drive crashes. Now you're talking about spending $200,000.

Let's say that you also want the application to interact with your external customers, which means that it has to be available all the time. Now you've got a whole additional set of variables. You will need redundant networks on the back end to make sure that if, for instance, Sprint goes down, AT&T can pick up the network traffic. And you'll need a disaster recovery plan with secondary locations, in case your primary location is knocked out by a flood or a hurricane. Now you're talking about spending $2 million.

All the while, the application looks exactly the same to everyone who uses it. You've gone quickly from spending $20,000 to spending $2 million—and nobody outside IT can perceive the difference. The users see an application on a screen, which is fine. But the C-suite needs to know the hidden costs.

If you're running an application for 20 people in a noncritical area of the business, then it's probably okay to spend $20,000 on a server.

If you're Jeff Bezos at Amazon, then you will probably feel okay about spending tens of millions on servers and backup technologies because your entire business model depends on 24/7 availability.

Just Like Buying a Car

Basing an IT spending decision on the user experience is like trying to buy a car without understanding anything more than the brake, the accelerator, and the steering wheel.

Here's what I mean: You can go into an automobile showroom, look at cars, and have a perfectly pleasant experience even if the only parts of the car that you are familiar with are the most obvious components. But that superficial knowledge will not enable you to make an intelligent buying decision.

At some point, the salesperson will ask you what kind of vehicle you need. Will you be using the vehicle for commuting to work or for traveling with the family to your favorite vacation destinations? Will you be using it to haul a trailer? Are you looking for a car that's fun to drive or one that feels comfortable and luxurious? Are you looking for a car with a big engine? Is good mileage important to you?

Most consumers can answer those questions easily. But you would be surprised at how few corporate executives can answer similar questions about their IT needs. The key to making competent IT spending decisions is a thorough understanding of what you really need.

Don't Forget Maintenance Costs

Ongoing maintenance costs are rarely covered thoroughly in discussions about IT investments. As a rule of thumb, I estimate that maintenance costs are equal to about 20 percent of the basic cost of an IT investment. Depending on the cost of the project, ongoing maintenance costs can add up significantly. Assuming 20 percent per annum, you are essentially repurchasing the project every five years.

I think we can all agree that maintenance is important. But the true cost of maintenance is often surprising. Make sure that maintenance costs are clearly spelled out in every IT investment proposal and that everyone understands why they are included.

The Math of Availability

How much you spend should depend on how much availability you need. You also have to know the real relationship between cost and uptime. Yes, there is some math involved—but don't worry, it's easy. Here is a series of hypothetical scenarios:

- If you need 99 percent availability—which sounds like a lot but means that your system will be down, on average, two days per year—your costs will be roughly $20,000.

- If you need 99.9 percent availability—what we call *three 9s*—your server costs will be roughly $200,000. You'll pay more, but your downtime will be reduced to about eight hours per year.

- If you need 99.99 percent availability—*four 9s*—your costs are now in the multimillion-dollar range. The good news is that you will only have 27 minutes of downtime per year. The bad news is that you will have to replicate every piece of data that enters the system. Everything—servers, discs, networks, locations—has to be redundant. If your business depends on constant availability, then $2 million will probably seem like a reasonable price.

- If you need 99.999 percent availability—*five 9s*—now you're talking about paying tens of millions of dollars for multiple servers, multiple locations, totally redundant architectures, and special applications that fail-over instantaneously with subsecond response time. If you're the FAA or NASDAQ, then it makes complete sense to invest tons of money in return for an average of only three seconds of downtime per year.

But if you're a regular business, then you really have to ask yourself these simple questions: How much availability do we really need, and are the costs justifiable?

To be fair, many businesses need all the availability they can reasonably afford. Here's why: In most cases, you cannot predict when the downtime will occur. If an outage occurs at an off-hour when there's little demand for the system, consider yourself fortunate. If an outage occurs at a peak hour during your busiest season, you might not feel so lucky.

Another example: Imagine that you need a business intelligence (BI) tool that runs on your PC, something that performs straightforward financial analysis. You can spend $100 for a copy of Microsoft Excel or a $1,000 for a copy of a more sophisticated piece of software from a dedicated BI vendor. Either way, you'll probably be fine—as long as all the data you need is sitting on your PC.

Let's say you want that same tool to analyze financial data from every business unit in the company. Now you need a data warehouse, specialized data management tools, applications for converting foreign currencies into dollars, data storage facilities, compliance software, network capability, and more.

Instead of spending hundreds or thousands of dollars, you're spending millions of dollars. From your perspective as a user, very little has changed—you're still using the same tool on the same PC. But your costs have escalated dramatically.

Here's another example: You decide to create a simple system for keeping track of your team's projects. You buy a server for $20,000 and you stick it under someone's desk. Twenty people use it. If someone trips over a cable and accidentally unplugs the server, it won't be the end of the world. That kind of scenario calls for 99 percent uptime.

Now let's say that you want to expand that same basic system to the rest of the enterprise. When you've got a system running across the entire company, you're not going to settle for two days of downtime per year. In fact, you're likely to want downtime measured in minutes, not hours or days. That scenario calls for 99.99 percent uptime. Now your IT investment is in the millions, not the thousands.

If you've ever wondered why IT spending as a percent of revenue varies by industry, the answer lies in the number of 9s you need to run your business. Manufacturing companies, which can tolerate days or hours of downtime, tend to spend 2 percent of their annual revenues on IT. Banks and financial institutions, which can tolerate only minutes or seconds of downtime, tend to spend 5 to 8 percent of their revenue on IT.

Those spending profiles add up to big bucks, and it's important for senior executives to possess a general understanding of IT cost trends for their industries. Most CIOs are aware of these trends. On the other hand, many executives who are not CIOs—but who nevertheless exert considerable influence over IT spending—are not aware of these trends. This gap in understanding is a primary cause of misalignment and friction between IT and the C-suite.

I personally believe that those kinds of misalignments and misunderstandings are largely avoidable. All that's needed is a willingness to look under the hood, poke around a little, and get a basic grasp of how the various components work.

My Favorite Analogy

I grew up in Michigan and graduated from Michigan State University. My first real job was at Ford Motor Company. Is it surprising that my hobby is collecting and racing cars?

Yes, automobiles are my passion, and sooner or later I tend to draw analogies between everything that I do and cars. I often find that the best way to explain IT concepts is by comparing them to cars. So please bear with me.

- A Honda Civic with a 200-horsepower engine costs around $20,000.
- A Porsche 911 with a 400-horsepower engine costs around $100,000.
- A Ferrari 458 with a 600-horsepower engine costs around $300,000.

■ A Bugatti Veyron with a 1200-horsepower engine costs around $1 million.

If you're commuting to work every day, the Honda is the clearly best choice. If you need to own the fastest and most sophisticated production car on the road, then you'll just have to buy the 16-cylinder Bugatti Veyron.

What's interesting to me is how the four examples of automobiles (Honda, Porsche, Ferrari, Bugatti) map nicely to the four levels of uptime (and corresponding levels of IT investment):

■ 99 percent uptime: tens of thousands of dollars
■ 99.9 percent uptime: hundreds of thousands of dollars
■ 99.99 percent uptime: millions of dollars
■ 99.999 percent uptime: tens of millions of dollars

It's not a perfect analogy, but you get the idea. The net takeaways are that you will pay for higher levels of performance and that you should only pay for what you need. Will vendors try talking you into buying more than you need? Yes, they will. It's your responsibility to resist the efforts of those vendors, and the best way is by knowing precisely which level of IT horsepower you need to keep your business running smoothly.

The Hard Facts of Uptime

In my experience as a CIO, I have found that many CEOs expect IT systems to be up and running all the time. This expectation is neither realistic nor cost effective.

The baseline for performance should be 99 percent uptime. Anything less than 99 percent is not acceptable. Occasionally I hear about an outsourcer providing 98 percent uptime. That's not okay; it's time to find a new provider.

But seriously, you might ask, why is it so important to understand these concepts? Here's why: The cost of uptime increases exponentially.

Suddenly what seems like a reasonable amount of money becomes a mountain of money. Don't let that happen!

You need to think in terms of how much unplanned downtime you can afford. The key word here is *unplanned*—because you never know exactly when the system will fail. Even if a system hasn't failed in years, some part of it will fail, or a human involved in the process will make a mistake. Either way, the result is downtime.

That being said, here are the basic hard facts of uptime.

One hundred percent uptime translates into 8,760 hours of continuous operation annually. Allowing for two hours of planned maintenance per week, the maximum annual uptime is 8,656 hours. A system with 99 percent uptime creates about 87 hours of unplanned downtime annually. That's a lot of lost productivity!

In truth, however, most systems with 99 percent uptime tend to be workgroup systems that are generally used during normal business hours. In other words, they are not expected to run 24 hours per day, 365 days per year. Ten hours per day, five days per week equals 2,600 hours per year.

That translates into two to three work days of downtime per year. Alas, you can never predict when a disruption will occur, or how much time it will take to repair it. A board failure with a four-hour response from a vendor is going to take at least eight hours to get fixed. A disk failure requiring a rebuild from a backup tape is going to take up to 10 hours to restore.

It is also generally assumed that a system with 99 percent uptime will not have a dedicated administrator or team of administrators. A system with 99 percent uptime will most likely become the responsibility of a "jack-of-all trades" who handles everything from PC support to video conferencing. If that person happens to be on vacation the day the system crashes, eight hours of downtime can rapidly become two days of downtime.

Ninety-nine percent is what you get when you buy an application, a server, an enclosure, and a battery backup; when your administrator is competent, but not an expert. Your investment is low—and your expectations should be on par with the level of your investment.

Increasing your uptime to 99.5 percent requires you to invest in Redundant Array of Independent Disks (RAID) technology that will preserve your data in case a disk fails. This dramatically decreases the probability of going to backup tapes to restore information. The additional complexity of those systems generally increases your investment by 50 percent, but the extra dollars you pay enable you to reduce your downtime significantly.

Ninety-nine point nine percent uptime is a general standard for critical workgroup systems and for some enterprise-wide systems. For a workgroup system, 99.9 percent uptime translates into approximately three hours per year of downtime.

Ninety-nine point nine percent means you have a dedicated server administrator, and you have bought redundancy for the system. Multiple servers are deployed to minimize the chances of hardware failures, disk technology is used, and power systems including battery backup and generators are used to ensure that the platform stays up.

Ninety-nine point ninety-nine percent is reserved for mission-critical systems. Ninety-nine point ninety-nine percent represents fifty-one minutes of downtime per year. Because the costs of uptime are exponential, the increases needed to take a system from eight hours a year to fifty-one minutes are quite large. Every server needs to be redundant, you need double the disk space to write copies in real time, two network providers are needed to ensure that the network is up, and a generator capable of running for days without grid power is necessary. In short, the costs are very large. If you have a customer-facing system in which every minute of downtime represents a lost sale, or you have a system that affects every area of the company, spending the extra money might be a wise choice.

Systems beyond 99.99 are reserved for applications where any downtime is catastrophic. Now we're talking about businesses such as Amazon that rely on systems as their lifeblood, critical control systems in airliners, or trading systems. Those kinds of systems need to approach 100 percent uptime. All of those systems experience some downtime, but it is a rare event that is usually measured in seconds per year, not in minutes or hours. In any event, if your entire business depends on a system being available, or if lives are at stake, then cost is not a factor.

For example, the control systems in an airliner are triple-redundant. The software for each system is written by a different team, and a separate system polls the control systems to make sure they all agree. Even if all the control systems fail, the airliner has redundant humans (also known as pilots) who can override what the plane thinks it should be doing. As you can imagine, the cost of those systems is astronomical.

Here's the key takeaway: Senior management should understand the relationship between dollars and downtime, and then pay for exactly what is needed. Paying for 99.99 percent uptime for your print server is wasteful and foolish, but putting your customer-facing online ordering system in a 99 percent uptime environment could damage your reputation and result in a significant number of lost sales.

Understanding that there are massive cost differences involved will help you align your IT spending with expectations, and allow you to maximize the ROI of your investment.

QUESTIONS THE C-SUITE NEEDS TO ASK

1. What is the spending profile of other companies in your sector?
2. How much reliability do we need?
3. What's the real cost of downtime for our organization?
4. Does the cost of preparing for the worst outweigh the potential benefits?

CHAPTER 2

Why IT Projects Fail

EXECUTIVE SUMMARY

Almost all IT projects require teamwork and collaboration across multiple functional areas of the company. The success of an IT project depends less on technology than it does on managing a smooth transition from an old business process to a new business process.

Technology Is Not the Problem

It is not unusual for IT projects to fail. Some estimates put the failure rate as high as 90 percent. I think we can agree that a failure rate of that level would be considered unacceptable in almost every other part of a company. Why such a high rate of failure is considered "normal" for the IT organization is too deep a question to resolve here. So let's focus instead on a simple problem: Why do IT projects fail?

The simple answer is this: lack of adequate governance. That's it in a nutshell. IT projects don't fail because of bad technology. Almost every IT project I've ever worked on has relied on established, proven, and highly stable technology.

Technology is not the problem. *We* are the problem.

When I say *we*, I mean those of us who have not insisted on putting a robust IT governance process into place before agreeing to move forward on an IT project.

I recently spoke with Vallabh Sambamurthy, a global expert in digital business innovation and competitive strategy. Vallabh is chairperson of the Department of Accounting and Information Systems (AIS) at Michigan State University's Broad College of Business. He spoke to me about the link between governance and effective IT. Here is an edited summary of what he told me:

> As the deployment and use of information technologies becomes a strategic decision in most firms, CIOs must actively work to promote an enterprise-wide involvement in and appreciation of the strategic links between business strategy and capabilities and the opportunities available through information technology.
>
> While CIOs cannot make most of these strategic decisions, they play a critical role in catalyzing and facilitating IT-based innovation. Therefore, one of the significant roles of the CIO is to facilitate effective business–IT relationships through appropriate governance processes. Effective CIOs are great listeners, communicators, and influencers!
>
> Effective governance processes tap senior business leaders to provide their creative judgments about the business strategy–IT linkage, owning the major strategic IT initiatives and appreciating the value contributions of IT. Ultimately, governance processes facilitate trust and understanding about IT.

Communication Is Critical

My friend Susan Certoma is the president, capital markets and wealth solutions at Broadridge Financial Solutions. Before joining Broadridge, she served in executive posts at Wachovia, Goldman Sachs,

Merrill Lynch, Lehman Brothers, and Credit Suisse First Boston. Susan knows IT *and* she knows corporate governance.

From Susan's perspective, good governance is built on a foundation of good communication. When IT and the various business units are talking the same language, it is easier to attain—and sustain—the alignment that is a prerequisite for great execution. A good part of the battle, says Susan, is learning how to speak in terms that the business will understand.

Susan told me a wonderful story about a senior executive who did not see the need for a governance process to oversee a proposed $750 million IT project. "What if the project was a $750 million business acquisition?" asked Susan. The executive saw her point, and agreed that having a governance process made sense.

Governance meetings can also provide good opportunities to help other executives understand the complexities of IT projects. For example, there is a tendency for senior management to treat IT projects like construction projects. But IT projects are not like construction projects. Unlike construction projects, which involve finite amounts of material, IT projects often involve millions of lines of software code. Those lines of code are written by teams of software developers. Being human, those developers make mistakes, and sometimes it is hard to detect those mistakes until later in the process. Moreover, there is a huge difference between writing software code and laying bricks or pouring concrete. Writing code requires creativity, insight, and flashes of inspiration. All of those factors create uncertainty. (A more detailed discussion of software development can be found in Chapter 6.)

"You can't look at a five-year project and give someone exact numbers," Susan explains. "It's better to sit down with the business leaders and show them a range of uncertainty. The uncertainty will be less in the initial years of the project and increase in the later years. The longer the project, the higher the uncertainty will be."

For Susan, good governance depends very much on good communication. But good communication with the C-suite is not enough—the C-suite also has to communicate its decisions effectively to the other levels of management. In other words, senior management should make the governance process as transparent as possible so that everyone in the company understands how and why decisions have been made.

The goal is avoiding what Susan calls "the great divide," which occurs when a company has a governance process but nobody outside the C-suite knows about it. "Governance should ripple down from executive management to middle management," says Susan. "It's not enough for the top executives to understand. The middle managers also need to understand the governance process."

IT Projects Are Really Business Process Change Projects

Here's why governance is absolutely essential: Almost every IT project involves changing a business process. Strictly speaking, IT handles very few "IT projects." The vast majority of projects undertaken by IT are business process change projects. The truth is that life would be much easier if we just stopped using the term *IT project* entirely and replaced it with *business process change project*.

That change in nomenclature isn't likely to take root any time soon, but it's important for executives to understand the key difference between an IT project and a business process change project.

An IT project is something like upgrading a server or replacing a bunch of network cables. A business process change project is something that impacts all or parts of the business. A business process change project is less about changing technology than it is about transforming the way people work. And usually, by the way, the transformation is permanent.

Referring to projects that are really about transforming business processes (and the behaviors associated with those processes) as "IT projects" creates dangerous misperceptions. When you call something an "IT project," people automatically tend to assume that most of the heavy lifting will be done by the IT organization.

Again, the best analogy here is the iceberg. The technology component of an IT project is like the tip that you see sticking up above the surface. The business process transformation component is the vast mountain of ice below the surface—that's the part that most people don't see, at least not at the beginning of the project.

When most people think of IT governance, they think of financial oversight and fiscal responsibility. Those are important parts of the IT governance process, to be sure. But the primary reason for having an IT governance process is to create opportunities for senior management to "see" the whole iceberg and not just the tip.

It helps to think of IT governance as a system for learning and a process for sharing knowledge. It's not just about looking at costs—it's a system for figuring out whether projects are really worth doing.

I hope that I'm not coming across as some kind of governance fanatic, because I'm not. But I know from experience that when IT projects fail, it's usually because of misunderstandings over cost, scope, timing, and expected results. A solid IT governance process will make it less likely for those kinds of potentially harmful misunderstandings to arise.

Let's return for a moment to the idea of transformation. As we all know, any kind of transformation has a minimum of three dimensions: people, process, and technology. Unless you take all three dimensions into account, the chances of your project succeeding will be exceedingly small.

Again, I would say that there is no such thing as an "IT project," because that makes it sound as though you can achieve a business result purely through the application of some new technology. In real life, it rarely works that way.

For example, let's say that the company decides to automate its manufacturing processes. Making the project successful will require close coordination among multiple departments and across several lines of business. IT will be a major player, no doubt, providing expertise and leadership. But it would be highly unwise for the company to think of the project as an IT project—after all, how much does IT really know about manufacturing?

To be successful, IT must work closely with the people in the departments and units whose processes are being transformed. IT cannot "go it alone"; it must act in partnership with the other parts of the enterprise.

When You Change a Process, Don't Forget the People

If there's one thing that most people really hate, it's change—any kind of change. Human beings are hard-wired to resist change. We are biologically programmed to dislike change. Humans like change about as much as cats like water.

I know, you're probably thinking, "I already know this." We have all been taught that people resist change. But when we're planning a business process change project, we become immersed in the technical details of the project. Those details become addictive, and they make us forget that the project isn't the new technology—the new technology is merely what enables the project.

Getting caught up in technical details of a project can be mesmerizing. It can become a distraction that prevents us from focusing on what's really important, which is the process change.

When you focus on the process change, you cannot help but confront the issue of fear. People are afraid of change, even when it offers clear benefits. If you don't take that fear into account, your project is more likely to fail.

People are creatures of habit. Interfering with their habits is like kicking over a beehive. Be prepared for a lot of angry bees!

Paradigm Shifts Are Real

We've all heard the term *paradigm shift* so often that it has become almost meaningless. But just because it seems old-fashioned doesn't mean that it's no longer a valid concept. A paradigm is a pattern or model.

It can be a set of standard practices and behaviors. In other words, it can be a set of habits.

When you implement a process change—in a department, an operating unit, or across the entire enterprise—it's a paradigm shift. You're changing the standard model and disrupting the established pattern. You're declaring a set of deeply ingrained habits to be obsolete. You're upending the status quo, rocking the boat, and kicking over the beehive.

Be prepared for the backlash. Chances are good that it won't be pretty. Some people will react irrationally because they are afraid. Everyone, fearful or not, will require guidance and support. Remember, you are forcing them to deal with a paradigm shift, and paradigm shifts make people uncomfortable.

Why is that so? The reasons are many and complex. Thomas S. Kuhn, the author of *The Structure of Scientific Revolutions*, refers to work performed by researchers operating within a paradigm as "puzzle solving." There's nothing wrong with puzzle solving—various types of puzzle solving are central to many tasks in modern life. But as Kuhn observes, "Perhaps the most striking feature of the normal research problems . . . is how little they aim to produce major novelties, conceptual or phenomenal."

The main purpose of most science, he notes, is adding to the "scope and precision with which the paradigm can be applied." In other words, when you're operating within a paradigm, your primary job is solving puzzles that fortify or refine the paradigm. Puzzle solving assumes that a solution can be found within the paradigm and that the act of puzzle solving is first and foremost a test of skill, and not necessarily a test of imagination, creativity, or originality.

As a result, puzzles without solutions are considered to be beyond the normal range of activity. By definition, they exist outside the paradigm. "It is no criterion of goodness in a puzzle that the outcome be intrinsically interesting or important," writes Kuhn. "On the contrary, the really pressing problems, e.g., a cure for cancer or the design of a lasting peace, are often not puzzles at all, largely because they may not have any solution."

Paradigms provide us with structure and comfort, even as they limit the scope of our activity and disincline us towards creativity. What does all of this have to do with IT? Plenty! Every time IT introduces a new technology, it's also introducing a new paradigm. It happens so often that we don't even see it as novel or extraordinary—that's precisely why the term "paradigm shift" has become a cliché.

But the fact that it's a cliché doesn't mean that you can ignore it. "Puppy love" is also a cliché, but knowing that won't help you comfort a heartbroken teenager.

Here are the two main takeaways from this discussion:

1. If you attempt to change the way people work without helping them transition through the change, they will fight you tooth and nail. The likely result will be a project that fails to deliver on expectations.
2. When departments or units try to implement projects in isolation or without consultation and collaboration with other parts of the enterprise, the likelihood of failure increases dramatically.

In today's economy, C-level corporate officers must take both of these points into consideration and develop practical IT governance processes that counterbalance the characteristics of human nature that tend to impede innovation and transformation.

QUESTIONS THE C-SUITE NEEDS TO ASK

1. Does the organization properly prepare people for business process change initiatives?
2. Are people being honest with themselves about the high failure rate of IT projects?
3. When new technologies are brought into the organization, does the CIO explain how they are likely to impact current business processes and established routines?

CHAPTER 3

The Washington Principle

EXECUTIVE SUMMARY

George Washington knew when to dive into the details of a problem and when to step back. IT governance is a process for making sure that the details are covered and thoroughly understood by all stakeholders. If Washington was alive today, I am certain that he would appreciate the need for good IT governance.

The Skills of a Leader

It's an understatement to say that George Washington was a great leader. He was an *exceptional* leader. He was also one of those rare individuals who can listen to the opinions of others without wavering from his true course.

In his role as commander-in-chief of the revolutionary army, Washington was surrounded by strong-willed, proud, and often egotistical men. Many of his subordinates were genuinely brilliant, and many of them had been successful entrepreneurs or seasoned soldiers before joining the revolutionary cause.

Washington's senior officers and advisors were self-confident, experienced, knowledgeable, and accustomed to getting their way.

They truly believed that they knew what was best, and they weren't afraid the share their opinions.

To many, Washington's management style seemed mysterious and mortifying. He would listen with the courtesy of a gentleman. He refrained from indicating his agreement or disagreement. To some, he seemed removed or aloof. To others, he seemed the embodiment of patience.

Many of his officers believed that Washington had *too much* patience. Some perceived him as indecisive. Some even accused him of being a coward.

History, of course, shows us that they were wrong. But imagine how extraordinarily difficult it must have been for Washington to preside over a group of senior officers that included Horatio Gates, Charles Lee, Benedict Arnold, Nathanael Greene, Henry Knox, Israel Putnam, "Mad" Anthony Wayne, and Alexander Hamilton.

Most of them, notes the historian Richard Brookhiser, had their own ideas about strategy. Each was undoubtedly convinced that his strategy would win the war.

In *George Washington on Leadership*, Brookhiser writes: "Every ambitious, self-confident person around a leader—including the leader himself—has a plan. And since every such person has some degree of talent or intelligence (otherwise they wouldn't be so close to the top), every one of their plans looks good, or at least reasonable. Picking a strategy is a trek among plausible options."

Brookhiser reminds us that Washington and his colleagues "had a half-dozen possible strategies . . . The fate of their country depended on making the right choice, but choosing was difficult because every strategy was good."

Some favored economic warfare, while others favored a strategy of evasion and harassment. Various forms of defensive strategy were suggested and considered. Strategies of maneuver, attack, and retreat were recommended, discussed, and debated.

Through it all, Washington maintained his stance as a keen listener and patient judge. He did not rush to a decision. As Brookhiser observes, "With the fate of the army, and the country, on his shoulders, Washington was willing to take an extra moment."

Indeed, it is fair to argue that Washington's patience was in large part responsible for winning the war. His patience was no doubt buttressed by his belief in a simple overarching strategy: Win the war.

When you have your own strategy, listening to others and taking their advice into consideration is relatively easy. That is the main lesson we can draw from Washington's approach to leadership. Listen to the people around you, consider their recommendations, and stick to your strategy.

I know that it might seem incongruous to compare winning the Revolutionary War to running a corporation. But I think we have all had days in which we wished that George Washington was around to help us make decisions. Maybe in the future there will be a Washington app that we can download to our smart phones. Until then, we will have to rely on our own best instincts.

In general, it seems that companies with simple, overarching strategies are successful over the long haul. Toyota's strategy was becoming the world's leading manufacturer of automobiles. Apple's strategy is designing beautiful devices that also deliver extraordinary value. These strategies have strong parallels to the struggle for independence.

Why We Need IT Governance

In most companies, IT governance is a four-letter word. It evokes images of long, boring meetings on subjects that don't seem particularly interesting to most people.

Washington knew the importance of governance, and he understood why it was important part of winning the war. While his generals proposed bold plans, Washington focused on what seemed to be trivial details. He reviewed food supplies and clothing, reviewed powder levels, and evaluated the impact of the army's movement on supply lines.

He realized that while these details wouldn't in themselves win the war, failing to address them would surely result in defeat. I think the same principle is at work in IT governance. It might not be exciting, but it is a necessity. Failure to address it will not lose a battle, but it might cost you the war. How many "brick and mortar" companies lost not to their chief rival but to Amazon or eBay?

A Process for Generating Commitment

IT governance provides a natural antidote to fear and resistance to change. IT governance is also a good business practice that yields positive results. In my experience, the difference between successful IT projects and unsuccessful IT projects usually boils down to business commitment. IT governance is the best way for generating the kind of business commitment required for guiding IT projects from conception through successful completion.

Today, all business leaders are required to make critical decisions about the role and value of new technologies. Despite the accelerated pace of business, please resist the urge to make rushed or injudicious decisions about IT investments. Poor decisions can be expensive to fix and often result in lost time. Lost cash can be recouped, but lost time is lost forever.

It's helpful to think of IT governance as a process for making absolutely certain that the company's key executives and managers meet together and say, "This is what we're going to do—are we in agreement?"

From my perspective as an experienced corporate CIO, the idea of people coming together to discuss capital projects makes complete sense. That being said, I am astonished and somewhat saddened by how few CIOs seem to meet regularly with the key influencers and decision makers in their companies to talk about IT projects. It's not surprising that so many IT projects fail.

Meeting periodically with senior management to talk about IT is a major challenge for many CIOs. Close working relationships with peers are prerequisites for success in most business scenarios, but for some reason, many CIOs find this part of the job difficult.

This I can state with absolute certainty: The CIOs who have the best and most productive relationships with their C-level peers are often the ones who have developed and maintained the best IT governance processes.

In business, almost everything depends on some kind of process. Why should IT governance be the exception to the rule?

At Terex, we had a strong governance process, and our ERP implementation had been fairly successful. Executives from other companies often ask me, "How are you guys able to pull off a global single instance, across multiple geographies, with all of your manufacturing, engineering, purchasing, and financial processes? How can you pull all that stuff together in a company that is so very diverse?" My answer is that we have a strong governance process.

When we started our ERP project, we had two-hour meetings with the COO, the CFO, and the segment presidents every Monday. We went through the details. We had lots of discussions, and a result, we had relatively few misunderstandings.

The first order of business for our governance group (which we called the Executive Steering Team) was to decide what business functions we should automate. An ERP system is a collection of modules that support functions like accounting, sales, human resources, supply chain, and manufacturing. During one of our weekly governance meetings, we asked the COO and the segment presidents, "Are we launching a financial system, or are we going to launch a closed loop ERP system where sales, purchasing, and manufacturing are all connected?"

At other companies, that question might have been resolved by IT, and IT might have chosen the solution that made the most sense from a technology perspective. But that kind of decision should be a business decision, not an IT decision.

We chose to implement a complete ERP system, meaning that every aspect of the business would be affected. It also meant that the implementations would be more complex and take longer to complete. While the cost and complexity were higher, the benefit to our customers and shareholders would be greater. A customer placing an order would know when the product would be built, and the purchasing organization would have global visibility into the supply chain and could then optimize spending.

Our experience illustrates the value of governance. Our choices were not obvious choices. Many companies take different paths when faced with those kinds of decisions. We weighed the trade-offs and made the right decision for Terex.

Sure, it took additional time, and nobody liked having another meeting on their schedule. In our case, however, the time and effort were solid investments that paid great dividends and created a shared purpose between the business and IT.

I am convinced that our weekly two-hour governance meetings were critical to the project's success. After the ERP project was largely completed, we cut back to holding governance meetings on a monthly basis. But our experience taught us that our time was well spent, and our monthly meetings continue to generate value for the company.

It hurts me to say this: When I mention those meetings to my CIO peers at other companies, they are often amazed. A typical response is, "That sounds great, but I'm lucky if I get an hour with the senior leadership once a quarter."

No wonder so many of their projects fail. How can IT align itself with the business—and remain aligned with the business—if the CIO only meets with company leaders every three months? To me, that kind of situation doesn't represent a failure of IT—it represents a failure of corporate management.

The difference between success and failure in modern competitive markets is often defined by the ability of the enterprise to align all of its various parts. That alignment does not occur magically; it's the result of a methodology and a process. A robust IT governance process can provide the enterprise with a genuine competitive advantage, because it's a great mechanism for achieving and maintaining alignment across the enterprise.

They Cannot Read Your Mind

I'm fairly sure that IT governance is not routinely taught or discussed in business school. Unless they have personally seen the value of a practical IT governance process, most managers and executives are not likely to immediately perceive its value. So the CIO or the CFO will need to figure out an effective and diplomatic way of educating the company leadership team.

You cannot expect people to intuitively grasp the necessity for IT governance. Most people do not consider IT governance an especially sexy topic—until you lay out the benefits of having an IT governance process and explain the dangers of not having one.

When I'm talking with people who need IT projects, but who aren't familiar with IT governance and who expect the IT group to just "wing it," I usually begin by saying something like this:

> 90 percent of IT projects fail. They don't fail because of technology; they fail because IT and the business are not aligned. If you want this project to succeed, IT and the business must be aligned. IT governance is a process for achieving that alignment. I need your commitment to that governance process, or I cannot commit the resources of IT to your project.

That puts the ball in their court. If they're not willing to commit to a governance process, why should IT commit to implementing their projects?

As we all know, you have to pick your battles carefully, and the last thing you want is to be perceived as a perpetual naysayer. But you also have an obligation to speak the truth and explain what it will take to make a project successful. Many people assume that all it takes is money. They are wrong, and it's up to you to find a polite and effective way of explaining why IT governance is critical to success.

My bottom line is this: IT projects are unlikely to succeed unless a robust IT governance process is in place—*before the project begins*. If you wait until after the project begins to align all of the moving parts, the chance of the project going smoothly drops to zero.

I'm sure that you've heard the story of the new CIO who finds three envelopes in her desk drawer. Inside the first envelope is a note that says, "Blame the previous CIO." Inside the second envelope is a note that says, "Apologize and take the bullet." Inside the third envelope is a note that says, "Prepare three envelopes."

There's a reason why the professional life expectancy of most CIOs is shorter than other C-level executives: Most IT projects fail.

Allow me to propose a different narrative: You can become the CIO who does *not* move forward with a new project until a governance process is in place. That governance should guarantee alignment among all the parts of the enterprise that are necessary to ensure success.

Make governance a nonnegotiable part of every project. Become the CIO who not only survives, but is promoted!

Multiple Levels of Governance

At Terex, our IT governance process actually had several levels. In addition to an executive group, we have governance teams within the business units and at multiple sites. Including a range of levels in the governance process reduces the chances of our overlooking or ignoring something that might jeopardize the project.

This is an important concept that many companies tend to forget: You need input, insight, and information from all levels and all areas of the enterprise. Inclusiveness and diversity aren't just buzzwords; they are essential for effective governance.

For example, a screen configuration that makes complete sense to a software developer might be totally impractical for a customer service rep. It's important to know these things before they become engraved in stone, or are written so deeply into the operating system that it would cost millions to fix them.

As experience demonstrates, the most valuable insight often comes from the people on the front lines. Don't forget to include them in your governance process—they can save you from making expensive mistakes!

Delivering Expected Value

Until fairly recently, it was common for executives to argue about the value of IT projects. From my perspective, I think that we've figured out how to answer the value questions. The issue now isn't determining or defining the value of an IT project; the issue is whether the project *delivers* the value that we expected. Have we achieved what we set out to achieve when we began the project?

When an IT project underperforms—does not deliver the value that was expected—there is an understandable tendency to blame IT. People say, "IT didn't deliver the value" or "IT didn't execute properly, and as a result we're not getting the value we expected."

But when I look at IT projects that aren't delivering their expected value, I usually see something else: Business processes that didn't keep up or weren't aligned with new technology.

I don't see technology failures; I see management failures. I see people who were unwilling or unable or unmotivated to change how they do business. (That is another good reason for the CIO to be thoroughly involved in the decision-making process; you need to make sure that the CIO has bought into the plan!)

As mentioned before, change makes people uncomfortable. Nobody wants to think that their previous experience might become irrelevant. Paradigm shifts are painful. People push back and become less productive. You hear people saying, "I've been doing it this way for the past 30 years, and I'm not going to change."

I witnessed this kind of phenomenon firsthand when I was at Ford. The first time we tried introducing lean manufacturing processes, we actually became less productive and less efficient. It wasn't that we didn't understand the potential value of lean manufacturing—it was clear to most people in the automotive business that Toyota was generating value from its lean manufacturing processes—but we didn't appreciate how difficult it would be to move from understanding value to delivering value.

We underestimated the complexity of the business process changes and the extraordinarily high levels of commitment that are required to make that kind of major transformational leap successfully. We were terrific at solving the puzzles confronting us within our existing paradigm. But when we tried to change the paradigm without first changing the business processes, we failed.

Fortunately, there's a happy ending to this story. When we brought the unions and the workers into the manufacturing transformation process, we were able to achieve the alignment we needed to start generating value from lean manufacturing. When we gained their trust, we also gained their knowledge, experience, and cooperation.

There's a lesson there for all of us. All change creates discomfort. The change doesn't have to be on the manufacturing floor—it can be anywhere. I still remember people complaining about having to learn how to use a mouse. They were comfortable with their green screens and their command lines, and the mouse seemed like some foolish new toy.

Always remember that when you take people out of their comfort zones, they tend to hunker down. You can't enter new markets, create innovative products, and beat the competition when you're hunkered down. So the real challenge isn't changing the paradigm; the real challenge is changing behaviors and attitudes. The best place to begin changing the way people behave and perceive the world around them is in the governance process.

Think of governance as the canary in the mineshaft. If your governance process is working, that's a good sign. If it's not working—watch out.

The Basics of Good Governance

Because I speak frequently about the need for IT governance, people often ask me to describe what a governance process should look like. My answer usually sounds something like this:

A basic governance process has three components: executive sponsorship, business ownership, and technical expertise.

Executive sponsorship is necessary to provide the clout or gravitas required to make things happen and ensure that people are paying attention. You don't always need a C-level executive on your governance committee—it usually depends on the scale of the project. If it's a small project, you can make do with a junior executive. If it's an ERP system that you're spending millions to implement, make sure you have one or two C-level executives on board.

Business ownership is necessary to ensure that the project will deliver real business value. I think of business ownership as the anchor that holds the project firmly in the real world. In most cases, the project is undertaken at the request of the business, so it doesn't make sense for the business not to participate in the governance process. In any event, the business unit that requests the project and develops the business case to justify the expense is the project *owner*. The IT group *enables* and *manages* projects. It doesn't own them.

Technical expertise is necessary to make sure that all the bases are covered and the details are worked out properly. When I use the term *technical expertise*, I'm not just referring to IT people. Many IT projects require input and advice from a variety of experts from different parts of the enterprise. It's not uncommon for me to seek input from diverse sources such as finance, legal, HR, product engineering, sales, marketing, customer service, and even facilities maintenance.

My basic belief is that the more you know, the better off you are, and the less you know, the more likely you are to make a mistake. That's why I tend to cast a wide net when I'm looking for expert advice.

A final comment before leaving this chapter: There is no right or wrong way to set up a governance process. The important thing is having a governance process in place. Let me share a story from my early days at Terex that illustrates my point.

I had recently become CIO and I had decided to structure the IT group by region to achieve economies of scale. It seemed like a completely logical idea, at least in theory.

But in practice, it turned out to be a bad idea. Terex is a segment-based organization, and my decision to structure the IT group on a regional basis resulted in a series of misalignments and misunderstandings.

If my decision had been discussed, reviewed, and vetted by a governance committee, the flaws in my thinking would have been exposed before the restructuring was implemented, instead of afterward. It took me a year to fully understand my mistake and fix it. Luckily, the damage wasn't severe and I learned my lesson without being fired.

Looking back on it, I am certain that a governance process would have spared everyone—including me—the trouble and expense resulting from my error. Friedrich Nietzsche said, "That which does not kill us makes us stronger." While I generally agree with him, I would hasten to add that good governance can help you avoid those kinds of nasty situations altogether.

QUESTIONS THE C-SUITE NEEDS TO ASK

1. Does the CIO meet regularly with other members of the C-suite to share ideas, review the status of existing projects, and discuss opportunities for new projects?

2. Does the IT governance framework ensure ongoing communication among C-level executives and key decision makers?

3. Does senior management follow "The Washington Principle" when planning IT projects?

CHAPTER 4

Balancing Risk and Exposure

EXECUTIVE SUMMARY

The best CIOs offer multiple options and choices. Establishing standard processes for measuring risk and reward makes it easier for senior management to assess the potential business value of IT projects.

The CIA Model of Risk Assessment

It's important for the CIO to have a standard process for balancing risk and exposure when prioritizing IT investments. It's equally important for the rest of the C-suite to understand the CIO's process for assessing risk, because the CIO cannot perform this function in a vacuum. The risk assessment process often requires knowledge from several functional areas of the enterprise, and it should be a team effort.

The C-suite and the CIO must work together to produce effective assessments of multiple risk/exposure scenarios. Collaboration is crucial because no individual or functional area of the enterprise possesses all of the knowledge and experience required to generate an accurate assessment. Ideally, your IT investment decisions will be influenced significantly by these risk/exposure assessments, so take the time to get them right.

Remember, it's a balancing act. No one can afford to protect everything all of the time. There will always be some exposure. The goal is determining which systems and applications are worth protecting and how much you should spend protecting them.

An Easy Method for Modeling Risk

The CIA risk assessment model has nothing to do with the Central Intelligence Agency or the Culinary Institute of America. In this model, CIA stands for *Confidentiality*, *Integrity*, and *Availability*.

Confidentiality refers to the level of secrecy required for the data in the system or application. For example, if you're storing Social Security numbers, you need a high level of confidentiality.

Integrity refers to the level of consistency and accuracy of the data held in the system or application. For example, you want financial data in your systems and applications to remain unchanged from day to day.

Availability refers to the level of uptime required for the system or application that's storing or processing the data. In other words, will the system or application be up when we need it? How important is it for the system or application to be up all the time? How much downtime can we afford? An example would be your online ordering system, where downtime could drive lost sales.

The Risk Profile Matrix

Earlier I mentioned that it's critical to perform accurate risk/exposure assessments. The good news is that they're not especially difficult— what's important is doing them, making them part of your normal routine. Let's work through some examples, and you'll see what I mean. In each example, we'll set up a simple 3 × 2 risk profile matrix, like this:

Confidentiality   **Integrity**   **Availability**

Then we'll assign values on a scale of three to one (three being the highest and one being the lowest) to the second row under each column.

For example, an application requiring high confidentiality, high integrity, and high availability looks like this:

Confidentiality	Integrity	Availability
3	3	3

An application requiring high confidentiality, medium integrity, and low availability looks like this:

Confidentiality	Integrity	Availability
3	2	1

Now let's dig a little deeper and look at some specific examples:

Let's say we're trying to figure out how much to invest in an application for making month-end reconciliations. Our risk profile matrix would probably look like this:

Confidentiality	Integrity	Availability
3	3	2

How do we arrive at those numbers? Well, we know that we need the highest levels of confidentiality and integrity. But we also know from experience that the world won't come to an end if the application isn't always available.

Now let's say we're trying to figure out how much to invest in an HR (human resources) system. Our matrix might look something like this:

Confidentiality	Integrity	Availability
3	2	1

Our HR system needs the highest level of confidentiality, but it's not essential for it to have the highest levels of integrity and availability.

Our external web site is another matter. Nothing on the web site is confidential, and large chunks of it are likely to be changed or modified on short notice. The only imperative is availability—it must be up and running 24/7 because it's a customer-facing system. So the risk profile matrix for our external web site will probably look like this:

Confidentiality	Integrity	Availability
1	2	3

Here's the likely matrix for a supplier management system:

Confidentiality	Integrity	Availability
3	3	1

Our supplier management system requires high levels of confidentiality and integrity. Since availability probably won't be an issue, why pay extra for it?

Our ERP (enterprise resource management) system is another story entirely. ERP systems require the highest levels of confidentiality, integrity, and availability. The risk profile matrix for an ERP system will look like this:

Confidentiality	Integrity	Availability
3	3	3

Okay, you get the picture. Step One is creating the risk profile matrix and filling in the variables. Step Two is calculating the downside risk—in other words, how much will it cost the company if something goes wrong?

Let's look at the example of the supplier management system. We rated the need for integrity at 3, the highest level, because we don't want information about our suppliers changing. But now we need to ask ourselves two more questions:

1. What are the odds that information in the system will change, either accidentally or willfully?
2. If the information does change, what's the impact on the company?

If it costs $10,000 to secure the integrity of the system, if the risk of someone or something changing information in the system is medium, and if your supplier costs are upwards of $1 billion annually, then the answer is easy: Spend the ten grand to secure the system.

But if the risk is low and your suppliers account for only a fraction of your spending, then maybe it makes more sense to invest your money somewhere else. I call this concept the Risk Probability Factor.

Do you always look at risk the same, or do you apply a Risk Probability Factor?

Not every situation will be as clear-cut as that example, however. So you will have to do the math. Again, the math is fairly easy: Multiply the dollar value at risk by the probability of something bad happening.

For the supplier management system, the value at risk is $1 billion and the risk of fraud is generally put at 1 percent. 1 billion x .01 = $10 million.

Is it worth spending $10,000 to insure the company against a potential loss of $10 million? I would say yes.

Here's how I would assess the risk/exposure scenario for the supplier management system:

Risk profile: Medium

Magnitude of Downside Risk: High

Cost of Solution: Low

Go/No Go Decision: Go

Here's another scenario: Several years ago, a good friend of mine was the IT director at a large company that took great pride in having a consistent approach for managing its IT assets. Among those various assets was a system for keeping track of when machines in the company were oiled. I think we can agree that a risk profile matrix for that system should look like this:

Confidentiality	Integrity	Availability
1	1	1

But here's the rub: The company had a strict policy requiring a password with a minimum of six digits for every system in its IT portfolio. It cost the company $500,000 to modify the software in the system that kept track of when the machines were oiled. The cost of securing that system far outweighed any potential risks. In fact, securing the system cost more than the system itself!

This story illustrates why broad edicts are generally a bad idea, and why it's important to have a straightforward process for analyzing risk at a relatively granular level.

It also illustrates why it's critical for the C-suite to understand the reasoning behind IT investments. Let me share another brief story with you, one from my own career.

When I joined Terex in 2006, the company had a local data center for its corporate group. The data center supported the financial systems we used to reconcile our books. The CEO's files were also stored in the data center.

The data center did not have a backup generator. We had battery backups and systems in place that would preserve the data in case of a power failure, but I couldn't guarantee full availability of the system if a severe thunderstorm or hurricane knocked out the electricity for a couple of hours.

And that bothered me. As the head of IT, I was responsible. So I went to Phil Widman, our CFO, and told him that I wanted to spend $250,000 on a backup generator. Phil turned down my request. He didn't see this as a good use of capital.

My sense of anxiety did not go away. Sure enough, a storm hit the area six weeks later. The storm knocked over dozens of trees, several of which fell against utility wires. Exactly as I had feared, the data center lost power. Adding insult to injury, the outage occurred on the very day when we were reconciling our books.

I was certain that I would be chewed out, or worse. I spoke to Phil and gave him minute-by-minute updates on the repair work performed by our local utility company. I told him, "This is why I wanted the backup generator!" He just looked at me and smiled. I asked him if the storm had changed his mind about buying the generator.

His answer was simple and elegant: "No, Greg, we are not going to buy the generator for the same reason that we didn't buy the generator six weeks ago. Losing power is an inconvenience. But losing power is not costing us $250,000. We're not going to spend $250,000 to fix a problem that we don't have. We will reconcile the books when the power comes up tomorrow, and our CEO will manage without his files for a couple of hours."

Phil's response taught me a crucial lesson—he really walked the talk. He understood how to find the right balance between risk and exposure, and he stuck to his principles. To me, the storm seemed like a worst-case scenario. To him, the storm was an irritation, not a cause for panic.

The bottom line is that you have to know the value of the asset you're trying to protect. You can't always determine that value based on your own assumptions. That's why the executive suite needs a repeatable process for making decisions about IT investments.

Making this process routine, standard, and habitual will prevent you from buying a Porsche when all you really need is a Honda, buying a Honda when you really need a Ferrari, or buying a Ferrari when you really need a Bugatti!

I believe that it is the responsibility of the CIO to explain this process to the rest of the C-suite. Don't assume that everyone will just "get it." Take the time to review the process in face-to-face meetings. Your colleagues will genuinely appreciate the effort, and the company will benefit in the long term.

Bring Options and Recommendations to the Table

For a deeper dive into IT risk management, I reached out to an expert, Kelly Bissell. Kelly leads Deloitte's Information & Technology Risk Management and the Global Incident Response practices. In 2012, they performed 457 projects across all industries, helping clients deal with challenges such as cybersecurity, identity management, breach incident response and forensics, privacy and data protection, IT risk management, secure development lifecycle, enterprise resiliency, and emerging security risks.

Kelly has more than 25 years of IT experience. He's been with Deloitte for more than ten years, and he helped build the security practice from a handful of practitioners in 2002 to the global practice it is today. Kelly has also performed 17 merger and acquisition (M&A) due diligence projects. I think it's safe to say that he really knows his way around a balance sheet!

I asked Kelly to describe what he sees as the major challenges facing C-level executives who are responsible for making critical decisions about IT investments.

"Every company is different, and a lot depends on the type and life stage of the company," says Kelly. "The challenges facing start-ups are different from those facing long-standing firms. Companies in high-growth mode or acquisition mode have different challenges than companies in cost-cutting mode."

Despite those differences, the role of the CFO is generally a constant across industries and life stages. "CFOs are held responsible for managing the funds of the company. When the CIO brings up a proposal for an IT project, the CFO needs to understand the rewards and the risks involved with going forward with that project. The CFO also needs to know the risk of not going ahead with the project. In other words, the CIO has to paint a complete and holistic picture showing the likely outcomes if the project is approved, and the likely outcomes if the project is rejected."

Since the CFO's job is determining the actual business value of the project, it makes sense for the CIO to bring as much detail to the discussion as possible. We're talking about financial detail, not technical detail. If you are the CIO, the CFO will assume that you have the technical aspects of the project under control. It's important to remember that the business case for moving forward with an IT project should be made using the language of finance, not technology.

"The best CFOs want multiple options and clear recommendations," says Kelly. "If the discussion is about installing a backup recovery system facility, the CFO needs to know how much it will cost the company if there's a failure. The CFO also needs to know the probability of a failure occurring. Those numbers are critical to the CFO, and the CIO should be ready to provide them."

For example, let's say that your company's information is worth $9 million and it would cost $2 million to build an off-site recovery facility. At first, it might seem like a no-brainer to approve building the facility.

But what if you knew that the chances of the information being totally lost or compromised were practically zero? And what if you knew that in the event of a disaster, it would cost $2.5 million and two months of effort to recover a large portion of the lost information? Armed with that information, you might decide that *not* spending $2 million on a backup recovery facility that might never be used is a risk worth taking.

The problem is that many CIOs are not comfortable having those kinds of conversations with CFOs, CEOs, and board members. Many CIOs would greatly prefer keeping the conversation focused on technology. But as Kelly points out, technology is usually not the issue. When the C-level officers of a company decide to consider approving a project, they aren't thinking about technology—they're thinking about money.

"The CFO wants a range of options and a recommendation," says Kelly. "The CFO wants the CIO to show the various options for solving the business issue and the costs of moving forward, including the costs of doing nothing, and the chances of an event occurring. In my experience, I don't see many CIOs offering that level of detail when they present proposals for IT projects. If they did, they would bring a lot more value to the company, and they would earn more respect."

From Kelly's perspective, effective CIOs "translate IT-speak into finance-speak," and *really effective* CIOs "translate IT-speak into business-speak." That might seem like a subtle distinction, but it can make a huge difference. "When CIOs do that, they actually get fewer questions from top management," says Kelly.

I agree. CIOs who take the extra time to "translate" presentations into business language and who include a range of detailed options are generally perceived as more thorough and more trustworthy. Those kinds of positive perceptions can be worth their weight in gold.

Instead of merely reporting that a project is "on time and on budget," CIOs should consider presenting information in dashboard form, using KPIs (key performance indicators) and KRIs (key risk indicators) to show trends over time. Virtually all C-level executives are comfortable with dashboards, and they are likely to appreciate the CIO's effort to offer information in what has become a standard business format.

Managing IT Security Risks

IT security is another area in which CIOs should consider upping their game. "Most companies see IT security as a lock on the front door. But the front door isn't the real problem. That's because the bad guys are already inside," says Kelly. "I've seen statistics showing that 40 percent of security breaches take place inside the company."

Effective IT security doesn't just monitor and detect what's going on *outside* the company; it also monitors and detects what's going on *inside* the company.

"I lead breach response service for the firm. Time and time again, I see that companies aren't aware that their information is already being traded. There's a huge global market for stolen information—on the scale of about $11 billion. You need capabilities for monitoring the market and detecting whether your information is being traded. Then you can take action to prevent further losses. Just locking the front door isn't the answer. You've also got to watch the black market and be ready to act."

I'm glad that Kelly has articulated a more nuanced approach to IT security. CIOs tend to think in binary terms about security. You'll hear, "Facebook is a risk, so we turned it off." But that's not the right approach, at least not to my mind. IT risk management is a process, and like any thorough risk management process, it involves multiple controls. Sometimes that can be a difficult concept for CIOs to grasp.

"You need multiple layers of security controls to manage risk. You can't prevent it all the time, but you manage it to the appropriate level of tolerance," says Kelly. "Different industries have different levels of security risk tolerance. For example, the intelligence community's level of tolerance is very different than the retail sector's level of tolerance."

There can be multiple levels of tolerance within a single company. For example, a pharmaceutical company will have a far stricter set of IT security controls around its product and research data than it has around other kinds of data. A company that manufactures airplanes will have more layers of security around its design processes than its HR systems.

It depends on the value of your intellectual property, and where that property is located.

For instance, a natural gas and oil drilling company would likely regard information about its lease options as highly sensitive, since the information would definitely help competitors. The drilling company would place very tight controls around its lease information, even though leasing is not considered its primary business.

The takeaway here is that IT security is not a one-size-fits-all proposition. Your IT security strategy will depend on your industry, the value of your intellectual property, and the nature of your regulatory environment, since regulations will vary from industry to industry.

Back in the old days, thieves would steal goods from warehouses. Today they steal information from data warehouses. As a French novelist once wrote, "The more things change, the more they stay the same."

What about the Black Swan?

I hope that most of you have read Nicholas Taleb's excellent book *Fooled by Randomness*, in which he invokes the concept of the black swan as a warning against complacency. As Taleb notes, the idea dates back to the Scots philosopher David Hume and was famously rephrased by John Stuart Mill as the "black swan problem."[1]

For our purposes, the black swan problem boils down to this: Just because something hasn't happened in a long time doesn't mean that it won't happen again. The financial meltdown of 2008 has been called a "black swan" largely because so few people saw it coming.

I'm not suggesting that you dwell on the possibility of black swans—they're definitely out there, but they're also rare. I mentioned the black swan because it supports my overall contention that you can weigh the risks and exposures associated with IT systems, and then take action—or decline to take action—based on objective assessments, rather than relying on gut feelings or falling back on "Well, that's how we always do it around here," and then hoping for the best.

QUESTIONS THE C-SUITE NEEDS TO ASK

1. Are you accurately calculating the probability of adverse events when determining risk/reward scenarios?

2. Do you have a process or practical framework for mitigating data security risks?

3. When plans for new IT projects are presented, is a range of options or alternatives fully discussed?

Note

1. "No amount of observations of white swans can allow the inference that all swans are white, but the observation of a single black swan is sufficient to refute that conclusion."—John Stuart Mill

CHAPTER 5

Time Is the Enemy

EXECUTIVE SUMMARY

Time is the one resource you cannot replace. Once it's gone, it's gone forever. Delays are the number-one killer of IT projects. Do not allow internal bickering or internecine conflicts to delay the implementation of an IT project after it has been approved.

Riding to Nowhere?

A fable for your consideration: A man gets into a taxi in an unfamiliar city. He has $25 in his pocket. He wants to meet his friends at a trendy new restaurant in another part of the city, but he can't remember the address, and the restaurant is so new that he can't find it on the Internet. The driver, who doesn't take credit cards, meanders slowly through the city's dark and deserted streets, searching for the restaurant. As they drive, the meter is running. The taxi goes up one street, and then down another. The process is repeated, over and over. When the meter hits $25, the man tells the driver to stop, pays the fare, and steps out of the cab. The man is alone, lost in a vast metropolis. He never finds the restaurant, never finds his friends, and is never heard from again.

I like that fable because it illustrates a genuine dilemma facing companies as they struggle to complete IT projects. Like the man in the taxi, they run out of time before reaching their destination. They forget that when you have a fixed amount of money to spend, time is the enemy.

Here is how it plays out in real life: The CIO comes to the board with a proposal for a new IT system that will cost $3 million and take 12 months to complete. The board approves the project, but several executives on the board disagree on important details of the planned system.

Some executives, for example, believe there should be two separate systems: one for internal users and another for the company's customers. The CIO believes that one system can get the job done, and will cost less money to operate over the long term. The CEO and CFO nominally agree with the CIO, but they don't fully understand why the sales, marketing, and customer service teams would prefer two systems.

The project begins and for a while, everything appears to be going smoothly. But under the surface, problems are boiling up.

At the next senior meeting of the senior management team, the following discussion takes place:

CEO: How's the project going?

CIO: We're on time and on budget.

CEO: Great!

VP Sales: You know, I can't help but think that we should have gone with two systems.

VPMarketing: I feel the same way.

CEO: I thought we agreed that it would be more cost effective in the long run to implement a single system.

CIO: Yes, that's what we agreed.

VP Sales: I read that you can do these kinds of projects for half the cost if you go with a cloud-based service delivery model.

VP Marketing: The marketing team at United Brake uses a cloud-based system and they love it.

CIO: We looked into that, but the cloud vendors can't provide the service levels or the security we need.

VP Sales: That's not what I'm hearing.

CIO: Honestly, if they could, we would have looked more closely at a cloud option.

VP Marketing: I've been reading a lot about the cloud, and according to the articles I've read, cloud vendors now offer a lot more service and security than in the past.

CEO: Really? That's interesting. Maybe we should give the cloud a second look.

CIO: We can, but it would delay the project.

CEO: I think we can afford an extra couple of weeks. Let's investigate the cloud option, and see if it makes sense for us.

VP Sales: Good, sounds like a plan.

VP Marketing: Great, it's worth taking the extra time to poke around and ask some more questions. There might be a lot of options out there that we haven't really considered.

CIO: Okay.

CEO: Excellent. Good meeting, everybody. Thanks for your time!

Although certain details have been exaggerated, our fictional meeting is actually quite representative of the kinds of meetings that happen every day at companies all over the world. The VP Sales and the VP Marketing are clearly harboring a grudge. They were overruled initially, and now they're venting their frustration on the hapless CIO.

Even if the motives of the VP Sales and VP Marketing are completely benign, the debate over the project is wasting time. There's nothing wrong with a healthy discussion, but the time for debate was *before* the project was approved. After a project has been approved, funded, and scheduled, further debate or discussion is usually not helpful. It's not unusual for people to disagree, but when disagreements put projects in jeopardy, it's time for senior management to step in and remind everyone of their responsibilities to the company.

We've all heard the phrase "paralysis by analysis." Asking lots of questions and sending a project back to IT for "additional review" practically guarantees that a project will be delayed.

The CIO knows that every time the project is delayed, for whatever reason, the final cost of finishing the project will go up. Or worse, the project will run out of money and never deliver the value that was expected when it was approved. Suddenly it feels like we're back in the taxi!

So why doesn't the CIO speak up? There might be dozens, if not hundreds, of reasons. Let's just look at some of the most likely reasons:

1. CIOs see themselves as enablers. They provide critical services that help companies achieve their goals and objectives. They tend to be agreeable, because their primary role is serving the needs of other people in the company. They even refer to their colleagues as *customers*, which tends to foster "buyer–seller" relationships instead of true partnerships.

2. CIOs are generally technologists, and they tend to see the world in a different way from other people. As technologists, they know that finding the right answer can take time. They also know that in many instances, there is no right answer. When they don't know the answer to a question, they are likely to say, "I don't know, but I'll get back to you."

3. As a group, CIOs have low job security compared to other C-level executives. Their tenures are often brief. In general, CIOs are not looking to rock the boat, and they will avoid direct confrontations whenever possible.

In a perfect world, the CIO in our fictional meeting would not be so agreeable. The CIO would turn to the CEO and say, "Delaying this project for one month while I look into cloud options will cost the company $250,000 and push the completion date into next year. Is that okay with you?"

Let's say the CEO pushes back and says, "But what about the cloud?" In a perfect world, the CIO would say, "We've already looked into the cloud model and it won't work for this project. Besides, the discussion we're having today isn't really about the cloud. The reason we're debating this is because the VP Sales and the VP Marketing still don't agree with the board's decision to go with one system instead of two systems."

Now the CIO has put the matter back into the hands of the CEO, which is where it belongs. At this point, the CEO should step up and exercise his or her authority as final arbiter. I would hope that the CEO, after being presented with facts by the CIO, would make the right call.

Now let's return to the real world. It would be unrealistic for the CEO to expect the CIO (or any other senior executive) to state the case so plainly and directly. Clearly, it is the responsibility of the CEO (and in some instances the CFO or COO) to settle the dispute and make sure the project moves forward without delay. Any other course of action is irresponsible.

Always remember: Time is the real enemy. Delays, not technology issues, are the main destroyers of value in IT projects. That's why it's absolutely imperative to avoid unnecessary delays. In the world of IT, wasted time always translates directly into wasted money.

The problem is magnified with multiyear projects. Enterprise-wide IT projects can take many years to complete. Again, it's critical for top management to understand the real costs of delaying IT projects. Delaying a $25 million project for two or three months can easily add millions to its cost, and greatly reduce its value to the company.

There are also invisible costs. Do you really want employees sitting idle while executives bicker over projects? In addition to wasting valuable resources, stalled projects can lead to lower employee morale and reduced levels of performance.

Over the course of my career, I've found myself in situations where the only way to move the ball forward was by telling people the cold, unvarnished truth about how much their delaying tactics were costing the company. When you put the facts on the table, people will usually listen. I vividly remember telling a group of executives many years ago that their delays were costing the company $150,000 per day. Believe me, that got everyone's attention, and the project went ahead—without further delay!

Sometimes you just have to remind people that the meter is running and that you need to reach your destination before you run out of money.

It's All about Time

Many of you are familiar with the seven forms of waste identified by Taiichi Ohno, the legendary chief engineer of Toyota. A quick review of his list shows that almost all of them are in some way related to wasted time. Different translations from the original Japanese result in slightly different versions of the list, but the core meaning remains constant. This version is taken from *Lean Thinking* by James P. Womack and Daniel T. Jones:

1. Defects
2. Overproduction
3. Inventories
4. Unnecessary processing
5. Unnecessary motion
6. Unnecessary transport
7. Waiting

The authors add "design of goods and services that do not meet the needs of users" to the list. "Confusion and underutilized human potential" have also been added to later versions of the list.

The original list was central to the development of the Toyota production system, which we know today as *lean manufacturing*. I think it's fair to say that it's stood the test of time and proven its value as a management tool.

If it's been a while since you looked at the list, I definitely recommend taking a few minutes to review it. It's surprisingly easy to fall into the old traps that lead to wasted time, and I try to keep the list at the front of my mind when our IT department is working on a project. In addition to reading the classic *Lean Thinking*, I also recommend reading *The Toyota Way* by Jeffrey K. Liker.

If Necessary, Rebaseline the Project

Inevitably, circumstances will arise in which, despite everyone's best efforts, you run out of time and money before finishing an important project. That's when the concept of rebaselining is useful. In Chapter 8, we examine rebaselining in greater detail. For now, let's touch briefly on why rebaselining can be a practical option.

Rebaselining avoids the common trap of taking money from other projects to pay for a project that's run out of money, which is rarely a good solution. The first step in rebaselining is admitting that you have a problem and being totally honest about the situation. Go back to the board, the CFO, or the IT governance committee and explain the gory details, preferably in plain language without any techno-speak. Show them the choices and explain the likely outcomes of each choice. Get them involved—remember, management is a team sport, and everyone needs to be involved.

Rebaselining should be used sparingly. But when you need it, rebaselining is a practical approach for dealing with situations in which you've run out of time and money. It is almost always a better alternative than taking money away from other projects.

It's important to remember, however, that nobody likes surprises. If you're the CIO and you've been telling that board that a project is "on time and on budget," you cannot simply wake up the next day and ask them to rebaseline it. You need some kind of early warning system—a dashboard or a checklist—that will give you a heads-up when projects are at risk. You need a methodology for watching trends as they develop over time. The idea, of course, is spotting problems while they're still manageable and before they morph into potential disasters.

The 5 Whys

In many situations, the root cause of a problem is hidden or obscured. Getting to the bottom of a problem quickly can save time and money. The "5 Whys" technique used in Six Sigma is particularly useful when you need to solve a problem with minimal delay. In the fictional meeting described earlier in the chapter, the 5 Whys would have quickly revealed the true source of the problem, and the CEO would have acted swiftly to keep the project moving ahead briskly.

Basically, the 5 Whys is a simple process for identifying the root cause of a problem and outlining a workable solution. The process requires asking a series of increasing specific questions (usually five or six) that guide you past facile answers and take you to a place where you can really begin solving the problem.

For example, my friend Ted is a private pilot. He recently had to land his Cessna on a state highway. Fortunately, no one was injured. But the mishap was both embarrassing and expensive, since he had to have the plane's wings removed so it could be hoisted onto a flatbed truck and towed back to the airport. Let's apply the 5 Whys technique to Ted's problem and see if we can help him prevent another forced landing.

Question 1: Why did Ted land the plane on a highway instead of the airport?

Answer: The plane's engine stopped.

Question 2: Why did the plane's engine stop?

Answer: It ran out of fuel.

Question 3: Why did Ted take off without enough fuel?

Answer: He didn't know there wasn't enough fuel in the plane because he didn't visually inspect the levels in the plane's fuel tanks before taking off.

Question 4: Why didn't he visually inspect the fuel levels?

Answer: He forgot, because he didn't use a checklist.

Question 5: Why didn't Ted use a checklist?

Answer: He had fallen into the habit of not using a checklist before making short trips, and since he had only planned a short trip that day, he didn't use a checklist.

As you can see, by the time we reach the fifth question, we have a pretty good idea of the root cause of the problem and we're pointing toward a practical solution: Ted needs to use a checklist every time that he flies, whether he's planning a short trip or a long one.

I find the 5 Whys technique extremely helpful. It tends to keep me—and the people around me—honest when we're dealing with problems. Instead of focusing or fixating on the most superficial reasons for a problem occurring, the technique helps us see beneath the surface of the problem and find its root cause.

QUESTIONS THE C-SUITE NEEDS TO ASK

1. Are unspoken concerns or unseen rivalries delaying the implementation of IT projects?

2. Do all C-level executives fully understand the costs and risk associated with delaying IT projects?

3. Is there a process or mechanism in place for identifying problems that could delay or derail IT projects?

CHAPTER 6

Software Is Not Manufactured

EXECUTIVE SUMMARY

Software development is a creative process that requires invention. Even the simplest projects have unknowns. A new software development approach is necessary to meet the needs of the fast-moving modern business climate.

The Art of Programming

There is an unfortunate tendency among non-IT people to perceive software development as a manufacturing process. This tendency is understandable. We have inputs called orders, we have raw materials in the form of servers and PCs, and we have workers in the form of programmers who assemble the orders based on what options they want, and they do this to a particular timing based on the needs of the customers. The length of time it takes to complete an order—three weeks, three months—depends on the size of the order.

The perception that software development (SWD) operates by the same principles as manufacturing processes leads to mistaken assumptions, false beliefs, and disappointing outcomes. To be blunt, SWD is not a manufacturing process.

SWD is an engineering and innovation process. It is invention at its very core. By definition, anything that has to be developed doesn't exist. Things that don't exist are far less predictable than things that just need to be assembled. That's an extremely important concept that is often lost in the dialogue between business leaders and IT leaders.

Small SWD projects, such as creating a new report with a couple of additional fields, are relatively predictable. Small-scale projects that replicate commonly understood processes are easy to manage because most of the work involves reusing existing code. Unfortunately, however, most SWD projects do not fall into that category.

Most SWD projects require iterative steps of invention and testing. Testing is time consuming, but it is my belief that most failures of technology can be traced back to inadequate testing. In my experience, most problems can be caught and fixed with proper testing. I would argue that testing is a best practice that separates very good CIOs from average CIOs.

Oddly, when time is short, testing phases are often skipped or shortened. People cross their fingers and hope for the best. That is not a good strategy.

SWD involves teams of programmers writing thousand and often millions of lines of code. Invariably, there are errors. The rule of thumb is one defect for every ten thousand lines of code. Most of those errors are caught and fixed before the software goes into production. But even NASA, which has one of the best SWD teams in the world, copes with coding errors. NASA has driven its error rate down to two defects per one thousand lines of code, but the rest of us need to accept that errors will occur.

Our goal isn't perfection; our goal is finding the inflection point at which more testing isn't going to find significantly more defects. Good programming teams measure and monitor their work to understand where they are on the development cycle. They don't test too much, and they don't test too little. They find the right balance. Good CIOs know when it makes sense to take some risks to keep a project moving forward briskly and when it makes sense to do more testing, even if that results in a minor delay.

Software errors are a bit like typing errors. Even the best typists make errors. The simple truth is that the more you type, the more mistakes you will make. The same holds true for software code. The longer the program, the more errors it will contain. That is why you need to test software before it goes into production.

The following chart illustrates the danger of going into production with minimal testing.

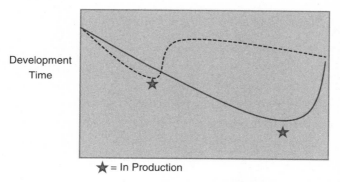

Development
Time

★ = In Production

Number of Defects Found

While the Dotted Line Project timeline shows that the project did launch with the customer significantly earlier in the cycle, it had more defects to fix after the customers started using the project leading to frustration and lost productivity. The Solid Line Project timeline shows an optimal launch. As the value of testing had bottomed out the project went into production. In both cases, a spike is noted right after the launch. This is typical of any project, because even as you try to account for how all users will use a product, there will be unknowns. Remember, SWD is mostly invention, not manufacturing.

Notice on the chart that the area under the curve for the Dotted Line Project is greater than the area under the curve for the Solid Line Project. In the chart, the area under the curve represents cost. Significantly more development time was devoted to the Dotted Line Project, which explains its higher cost.

Studies have shown that it is fifty times more expensive to fix a software error after the software is in production. Fixing a software error is like changing a tire; obviously, it's easier to change the tire while the car is in the repair shop than it is when the car is on the road. The Dotted Line Project was launched more quickly than the Solid Line Project, but the costs of fixing the errors were much higher for the Dotted Line Project. Additionally, when projects require multiple trips back to the drawing board, a certain level of frustration sets in, and that frustration can diminish productivity, which adds cost to the development process.

Is there a way around that dilemma? Many companies cave in and look to commercial off-the-shelf software (COTS) to minimize their SWD costs.

Many COTS solutions are now cloud based, and they have the advantage of being very quick to implement. But like anything that seems too good to be true, there are trades-offs.

Commercial tools are less customizable than in-house solutions. That means you will be changing your business process to match the software, instead of the other way around. A cloud-based HR software provider is not going to change its software to accommodate your unique performance review process. Instead, you are going to have to change your process.

To the CIO, that might seem like an easy decision. The cost of SWD drops, but the HR department has to develop a new business process. Depending on the circumstances, the right choice is not immediately clear.

Additionally, COTS solutions require developing connectors to a host of other systems, and the costs of developing those connectors can sometimes be much more expensive than the systems themselves. Imagine using a cloud-based HR system to keep track of employees. That system needs to be linked to the payroll system to make sure that current employees are paid, and that terminated employees are not paid. It probably also needs a connection to the accounting system. Already, we can see a host of "unknowns" that can drive up costs.

A cloud-based CRM system will create a different set of complexities. To make a CRM system work, you need a way to flow your sales data into accounting, purchasing, and manufacturing systems. All of those connections take time to build, and they cost real money.

An analogous situation would be a planned expansion of company operations into China. You could build a new facility from scratch, create a joint venture, or buy an existing company. What is the right answer? Most executives know there isn't a single right answer. There are too many variables. What if the joint venture partner is a competitor? How expensive would it be to buy an existing company in China? How long would it take for a new facility to become operational?

Software development is similarly complicated. One of the reasons that companies hire CIOs is to guide them through those kinds of complicated processes and decisions.

Consider Agile or Lean Methodologies

When an IT project is requested by the business, the request is usually the result of a perceived need by the business for a solution addressing an immediate business opportunity or competitive threat. From the perspective of the business, speed is absolutely essential.

Given that desire for speed, it is not surprising that conflicts arise between the business and IT over the pace at which projects are developed and launched. Typically, the CIO hears comments such as, "We need those projects now and you're taking too long to deliver them."

If you are the CIO and you're tired of hearing those types of comments, you might consider a new approach for developing IT projects. Expected value is typically identified up front, long before work on a project begins. The expectation is that every benefit laid out in the project will materialize, and that the project will be completed on time and on budget, costing neither a dollar more nor a dollar less than the amount budgeted.

For reference, this approach is called the Waterfall methodology (see the following graphic), and it was first introduced in 1956. It is a logical approach to designing projects, and the approval process is inserted after the requirements phase, but before the design phase begins.

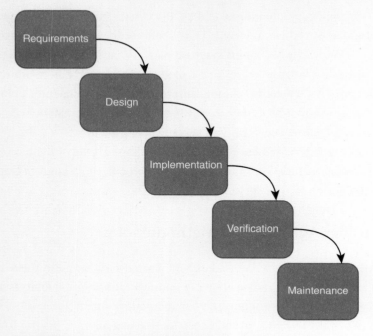

CIOs have an expression: "Quality, cost, speed—pick two." If you want it fast with quality, get your checkbook out, because you will probably need to engage a high-priced consulting firm. If you want to keep costs down, you can develop the project in-house with existing IT resources. If your appetite for risk is high, you can skip some of the testing, but the users will feel some pain.

The "pick two" attitude has its risks, and has led to the demise of many CIOs. A new approach is needed. Fortunately, there is a new way, and it has already proved itself in the real world.

The new approach is called the *agile methodology*. Like the lean methodology for manufacturing companies or Six Sigma for companies that require process control, agile changes the paradigm for thinking about how we create new tools. At its core is a one-piece flow concept in which work is pulled from developers, rather than pushed at them.

It also borrows from lean manufacturing the concept of Takt time, or cycle time. Short cycles are called Sprints, and they are the heartbeat of a lean development organization. Work is broken down into small chunks that can be delivered into typically two- or three-week intervals. Work is prioritized by customer input, and internal customers are part of the team testing in real time, not an output at the end.

Lean SWD methodology uses many new social media tools, including texting and videoconferencing, to interact with the users in new ways and to make sure that what is delivered is done right the first time. IT organizations that adopt lean methodology can see up to a 200 percent rise in SWD productivity.

All of the most successful software companies (e.g., Google, Apple, Facebook, Microsoft) use some form of a lean or agile methodology. Large banks, retailers, and energy companies have also been quick to adopt this methodology.

So why have we not seen this adopted across the board? I think the answer lies in the funding process for most companies. The funding process for an agile team is driven around constraining what you can afford to spend and then letting the work happen independent of projects in the financial sense. The work is still prioritized, but it is not tied to massive capital projects. It is tied instead to Sprints, which produce results in weeks rather than years.

QUESTIONS THE C-SUITE NEEDS TO ASK

1. Are you satisfied with the performance of software developed by your IT organization?

2. Does your IT organization use an agile methodology?

3. Is the business willing to dedicate some percentage of its resources up front to software development? In other words, does the business have "skin in the game?"

CHAPTER 7

Technology Disruptors

EXECUTIVE SUMMARY

Continuous transformation is the new normal. It's absolutely critical to stay current with new technologies that could upend or radically change the way your company does business. Don't get caught behind the curve.

Keep Your Eyes on the Horizon

No industry is immune from disruption. It doesn't matter whether your company makes steel or watches, sells pantyhose or power drills, distributes online video content or craft beers—some other company out there is waiting for you to miss the signals and drop the ball.

Disruptors often come in the forms of new technologies. But they can also arrive as innovative marketing strategies, novel approaches to distributing existing products, or new ways of extending credit.

As a senior executive, you are responsible for maintaining a sharp lookout for potential disruptors and having a plan ready when they appear on the horizon. The company's CIO can be a great source of knowledge about looming technology disruptors and can provide advance warning before they arrive full-blown on your doorstep.

If you are familiar with Clayton Christensen's books, you know what I'm driving at. In the preface to his famous book *The Innovator's Dilemma*, Christensen lists two basic management principles that often work against continuing success:

1. Listening to and responding to the needs of your best customers
2. Allocating resources primarily to innovations that promise the highest returns

As an executive and a steward of your company's resources, it can be incredibly difficult to ignore those apparently basic principles. But sometimes that is precisely what you have to do to succeed. What I would add to Christensen's foundational message is that in our rapid-fire economy, it's become more important than ever to know when you need to ignore the common wisdom and scan the landscape for outliers.

Disruptors can be especially problematic because the truly dangerous ones are rarely obvious. They don't appear with convenient warning labels, and they don't scream, "We're going to destroy your business model!"

Let's look briefly at three examples of disruptors that were largely dismissed as irrelevant—until they become dominant forces in their industries.

The introduction of the Toyota Corona was deemed irrelevant by U.S. automakers. The U.S. automakers derided the Corona and its smaller sister the Corolla as "rust buckets" with limited appeal. Worst of all, from Detroit's perspective, the Corona and Corolla were low-margin cars. The common wisdom in Detroit was that smart automakers focused on high-margin vehicles. As a result, Detroit paid little attention to Toyota. We all know how that story ends.

A similar disruption took place in the watch industry. Japanese watch manufacturers saw an opportunity to sell quartz watches at the lower end of the market. Swiss watchmakers ceded the market for quartz watches to the Japanese, who effectively used their foothold in the market to offer higher-priced watches that competed directly with the Swiss watches.

A more recent example is the spectacular success of the iPhone. The iPhone was famously dismissed as a novelty with limited appeal by top management at Research in Motion (RIM), which makes the BlackBerry. Again, we all know what happened next.

History is rife with examples of successful companies that were laid low by disruptive competitors. IBM, on the other hand, is an example of a large and successful company that has so far resisted being disrupted. IBM has accomplished this by setting up separate P&Ls within the companies for promising new technologies. Instead of forcing new technologies to run before they can walk, IBM carefully nurtures them until they are ready to contribute to the core business. IBM treats its potentially disruptive new technologies as startups, not as mature businesses. A different set of rules applies, and that makes all the difference.

Even if you don't want to set up a system for handling separate P&Ls within your business, you can isolate, protect, and nurture new ideas using what I call "strategic sandboxes." Basically, they are a management tool for parking new technologies until they are ready to be folded into your existing business or scrapped.

The sandbox approach enables you to maintain a stream of continuous innovation without a lot of cumbersome management infrastructure. In my role as a CIO, I used "strategic sandboxes" to test new ideas and run small-scale pilots involving new technologies. I found them quite useful, and recommend them as a standard management practice.

My guess is that the Google car—the driverless car that Google is developing—is a sandbox project. I don't think that Google expects it to generate cash for the company in the near future. What I do find interesting is that Google is driving the idea of the driverless car, rather than a major automaker like GM or Ford. If I were an automaker, I'd be keeping an eye on Google.

Think Like a VC

My friend Ross Kudwitt is CEO of two companies: Crisply, an innovative provider of employee time-tracking solutions, and Nine Summer, a software product development company. Ross says that CIOs should study the habits and practices of venture capitalists (VCs) and serial entrepreneurs.

"You can learn a lot from start-ups," says Ross. "Rapid prototyping. Failing fast. Using data instead of intuition to decide if a project is worthy of additional funding."

VCs know when and how to kill a project. They take the concept of "fast failure" very seriously. Instead of sticking with a project to the bitter end and losing $10 million, they know how to walk away from a doomed project after spending $1 million. Every successful VC develops the ability to determine when to pull the plug. I think that every CIO should have the same ability. When you know how to kill projects, you are less afraid to take calculated risks.

Innovation depends on taking risks. In modern hypercompetitive markets, innovation is critical to success. In the past, the CIO was expected to function primarily as a steward of the company's assets. Today, the CIO is expected to play offense and defense. It is a more complex role, but the game has changed, and the CIO has no choice but to adapt to the realities of a new playing field.

When Technology Disruption Hits Close to Home

From the CIO's perspective, it's critical to remember that technology disruption can occur within the IT department itself. In fact, in today's data-driven markets, IT can become ground zero for disruption.

Companies such as Salesforce are aggressively wrestling business away from traditional vendors. The cloud has become a battleground for a new generation of IT suppliers. The cloud's potential impact on IT is huge. A couple of years ago, analysts were still dismissing the cloud as mostly hype. Now CIOs are scrambling to adjust to cloud-based service delivery systems. An entirely new IT architecture is emerging, along with new technical standards and new pricing models.

With surprising speed, the cloud evolved into an essential piece of practically every company's IT strategy. For startups (which are the primary source of technology innovation), the cloud has become the de facto IT infrastructure.

There are striking similarities between disruption in the automotive industry and more recent disruptions in the software industry. Salesforce, for example, was seen as "CRM in the cloud," a niche offering that would appeal mostly to smaller companies. As a result, larger companies ignored Salesforce, or played down its potential influence. From their perspective, Salesforce was just another software-as-a-service (SaaS) vendor.

Within a remarkably brief span of time, however, Salesforce expanded its offerings to include platform-as-a-service (PaaS), which has the potential to become a much larger business. Innovative companies such as Workday have built IT platforms in the cloud with Force.com (Salesforce's PaaS offering), demonstrating clearly that the cloud is more robust than anyone had previously believed.

Like Toyota in the 1960s, Salesforce was seen as a niche player with limited appeal outside of specialty markets. And like Toyota, the company's potential as a disruptive force across an entire industry was largely overlooked. Two years ago, Salesforce was not seen as a serious competitor to established ERP vendors. Today, it is.

Technology disruptors can take many forms. And sometimes the threat isn't what you initially think it is. For example, when Netflix emerged as a competitor for Blockbuster, the general belief was that the Netflix's primary advantage was its delivery-by-mail model. You didn't have to visit a video store, and there were no late fees. But Netflix's long-term goal was eliminating the physical DVD and distributing movies online. If Blockbuster had perceived the true nature of the disruption, it might have responded more effectively to the challenge.

Blockbuster, in my opinion, could have used its scale to leapfrog over Netflix and establish an online distribution capability. Blockbuster saw only one part of the disruption, and not the whole picture. If they had seen the potential in online distribution, it might have gone on to become the Amazon of video content. Instead, Blockbuster is commonly cited as an example of a company that was outflanked by a more nimble competitor.

As I suggested earlier, disruptions are rarely "in your face" types of events. They don't announce themselves, and they can appear from almost anywhere. I think it's fair to say that the consumerization of technology has been a form of disruption. Who ever expected that consumer devices used at home by our families and friends would upend the way we operate in the modern corporation? Or that a phenomenon such as Facebook would define expectations for enterprise collaboration platforms?

Many companies today, including the company I work for, routinely use iPhones and iPads in the course of everyday business. When those devices were introduced, almost every CIO that I knew warned against using them. You rarely hear that kind of talk anymore. But that doesn't mean there wasn't a kernel of truth in their fears.

The fact is that new and potentially disruptive technologies are heading toward us all the time. I recently stood on line to buy one of the new Microsoft tablets. I didn't buy it because I am a raving fan of Microsoft or a dyed-in-the-wool propeller head. I stood on line because I know that if the new tablet becomes popular, our IT team will have to figure out the best ways to integrate it into our existing infrastructure and that we'll need to start writing apps for it. That's what I mean by keeping a sharp watch on the horizon—you never know where the next disruption will come from, and you need to be ready to pivot quickly.

For example, if Apple decides that the new Microsoft tablet is a threat to its market, it might develop a hybrid tablet that becomes the new standard. Then we would need to integrate it with our systems and write new apps for it. The cycles of innovation and adoption are accelerating, and there's no point in trying to turn back the tide. If tablets are becoming the new laptops, you need to begin preparing for the transition now. Get ahead of the curve. If you wait, you will fall behind and it will be harder to catch up.

Specific Trends to Watch

There's no question that cloud, social, mobile, and technology consumerization will continue as major trends with significant disruptive potential, at least for the next several years. I would also suggest keeping a close watch on big data analytics and gesture-based user interfaces.

Strictly speaking, big data has been around for a while. We've been collecting huge quantities of data and storing it in data warehouses for the past 15 years. So the idea of big data is not really new.

What is new, however, is the capability for extracting meaning from big data quickly and cost effectively. Until recently, you needed significant investments of capital to make use of large data sets. Now, thanks to massively parallel processing on commodity hardware, you can analyze large amounts of data very quickly and at a relatively low cost.

The term *big data* means more than just large volumes of data. When people talk about big data, they also mean the speed at which the data is generated (velocity) and the kinds of data being collected (variety).

Big data also includes unstructured data, which is the kind of data generated by social media (e.g., Facebook, Twitter), mobile texting, call center notes, security cameras, traffic sensors, and a legion of automated systems operating 24/7 all over the world. In the past, most companies were content to analyze highly structured historical data, which is the kind of data that can be stored easily in databases and data warehouses. Today, looking only at structured data would be considered looking at only a tiny part of a much larger picture.

Advances in big data technologies are opening a new frontier of predictive analytics that promises to revolutionize virtually every aspect of modern business. At minimum, it would be a good idea to begin developing some knowledge and expertise in this area, since the skills required to manage big data are different from traditional data management skills.

Beyond the Keyboard and Screen

User interfaces (UIs) are also likely to change dramatically over the next couple of years as touch screens replace traditional keyboards. You can expect to see more user interfaces that rely on sensing speech, recognizing gestures, and tracking eye motion.

Applications such as Siri just scratch the surface of what's possible, and every 18 months it seems as though someone declares the rebirth of artificial intelligence (AI). The talking computer on the starship *Enterprise* will soon seem less like science fiction and more like familiar technology.

The goal here isn't to predict what the future will look like but to prepare your organization to adapt to change, no matter what it looks like when it arrives. Somewhere in all that change is a competitive advantage—your job is finding that advantage and making it work for your organization.

Encourage Exploration, Experimentation, and Fast Failure

My advice to CEOs and other senior executives is this: Help the CIO create the "strategic sandboxes" that I mentioned earlier. Use those sandboxes to evaluate new technology on a small scale and determine which of the new technologies makes the most sense for your company. Leverage the CIO's technical knowledge and keep a steady watch on new technologies as they emerge. Rely on the CIO to be your "eyes and ears" for innovation. Ask the CIO to present regularly on the newest emerging technology trends. The CIO is uniquely positioned to see what's happening, and it makes good business sense to take full advantage of the CIO's knowledge.

Encourage experimentation and "fast failure." Reward innovative thinking and create a process for evaluating new ideas. Support a culture of continuous improvement and innovation. Try not to reject new technologies just because they don't come from traditional or familiar vendors. Reach out to experts beyond your company, and listen to their opinions.

Train yourself to keep an open mind, and try to imagine what the future will look like. Did anyone at GM or Ford envision what would happen to their companies if Toyota became a significant player in

North America? They saw the Corona and they laughed. They just couldn't imagine that the same company would compete against them at the high end of the market by selling a car called the Lexus.

QUESTIONS THE C-SUITE NEEDS TO ASK

1. Is your organization prepared to deal with technology disruptors when they arise?
2. Do you have "strategic sandboxes" in place?
3. Are you keeping an eye on competitors who will accept lower margins in exchange for a foothold in your market?

CHAPTER 8
The Office of Know

EXECUTIVE SUMMARY

In today's economy, collaboration is often an essential ingredient of success. The CIO and the IT team should be perceived as collaborators and team players. In the modern company, everyone has a strategic role; no individual or functional area stands alone.

Correcting a Classic Case of Misalignment

It's well-known across the IT community that the CIO is commonly referred to as "Dr. No," and the IT department is often called the "Office of No."

While it's not uncommon for some people and departments to have unflattering nicknames, those particular nicknames can make it harder for a CIO to establish the kind of rapport required to succeed as a C-level executive. Those nicknames also point to an intrinsically troublesome and potentially damaging misalignment between IT and other functional areas of the company.

In a recent conversation with my friend Mark Polansky, Managing Director of the CIO/IT Practice at Korn/Ferry International, a leading global executive search firm, he suggested that CIOs should work collectively on changing the "Office of No" into the "Office of Know." In the months following our conversation, I've given his advice serious consideration.

I truly believe that Mark hit the nail directly on its head. But I thought long and hard about whether it would be possible for CIOs to transform those negative associations into positive associations—without abandoning their primary responsibilities as stewards of an increasingly valuable set of corporate resources.

IT is expensive and mission critical. CIOs see themselves as guardians of valuable assets. In some respects, CIOs are like offensive interior linemen in football. Linemen are not generally expected to score touchdowns. But they make it possible for the quarterback, the running backs, and the receivers to execute the plays that result in touchdowns. When linemen do their job properly, they are invisible to all but the most knowledgeable fans. It's only when they mess up that anyone notices them.

Another part of the "Dr. No/Office of No" issue stems from natural differences between CIOs and other C-suite executives. In general, C-suite executives share many characteristics. I would describe most of the top executives I meet as intelligent, ambitious, energetic, self-motivated, self-confident, self-assured, social, successful, and responsible people.

Over the course of my career, however, I have noticed a handful of dissimilarities between CIOs and their C-suite peers. Some of those dissimilarities are subtle, and some are more distinct. For example, CIOs tend to believe more deeply than other C-suite executives that technology can provide solutions to most problems.

Another example: CIOs tend to be more risk-averse than their C-level peers. Sometimes, CIOs give the appearance of taking their responsibilities as corporate stewards just a little *too* seriously. There's nothing wrong with that, of course, but it can be off-putting in some situations. As we all know, sometimes even the subtlest hint of an attitude can be misinterpreted or taken amiss by someone else.

Are CIOs Wired Differently?

Does it feel as though we are treading on dangerous ground? Perhaps we are. But let's tread on. It's terribly important to understand the differences between CIOs and other C-suite executives. Far from being inconsequential, those differences are often the root cause of commonly held perceptions that IT underperforms or underdelivers.

I am absolutely certain that a rigorously scientific analysis of the DNA of a CIO and the DNA of a CEO, CFO, or COO would reveal no substantial differences. Nevertheless, different types of corporate officers behave differently, and those differences are consequential.

If you firmly believe that technology is the solution, then you are going to view the world in starkly different terms from someone who believes firmly that people and processes are the solution. IT people instinctively reach for the technology solution first. They do it because that's the way they're trained. It's a habit, and habits are hard to break.

If you're the CEO or the CFO or the COO, you shouldn't be surprised or disappointed that the CIO's first response to any problem is likely to involve a solution that relies on technology. That's just the way it is.

What's really important is the way in which you—the CEO, CFO, or COO—respond to the CIO's reflexive tendency to see technology as the answer to a problem. Sure, you can push the CIO into a corner by agreeing to a technology solution and then intimating that the CIO's job is on the line if the solution fails to deliver value.

If you take that approach, however, the CIO's risk-aversion habits will kick into overdrive. Instead of delivering a solution that guarantees success, the CIO will deliver a solution that avoids failure. From the CIO's perspective, the difference between succeeding and not failing might appear indistinguishable. From the perspective of the business, however, the difference can be huge. Here are three reasons why.

First, a solution designed to avoid failure is likely to be overly robust and needlessly expensive. Back in Chapter 1, we discussed the 80/20 Rule of IT spending. Uptime costs money. The more uptime you buy, the more expensive the project becomes. You should buy only as much uptime as you need. Buying more than you need is a waste of money.

Second, when you design a solution for maximum risk avoidance, you implicitly place the needs of the organization above the needs of the users. There's nothing inherently wrong with that, but you should be aware that you are making a choice with consequences. When users don't like a solution, they won't use it. The likely upshot: You wind up with an overly expensive solution that nobody uses, you blame the IT department for not delivering value, and the CIO looks for a new job at another company. Where's the sense in all of that?

Third, and most important, if the solution doesn't deliver the business value you had expected, you're essentially back to square one and you have accomplished nothing.

Sometimes the problem isn't the CIO or the IT department—the problem is top management. In those cases, the pejorative labels of "Dr. No" and "Office of No" become self-fulfilling prophecies and excuses for failure.

Sometimes There's a Good Reason for Being Risk Averse

Let me share two stories that illustrate why CIOs are risk averse. Like most CIOs, I often find myself responding to inquiries from other executives about social media and social collaboration platforms. They tell me about their friends at other companies, or they send me a link to an article they've read and then they ask me why we don't have a social media platform at our company.

That's when I find myself in the uncomfortable position of explaining how our competitors could easily gain valuable insights into our business plans by reading content posted by our employees. I also point out that when we post our proprietary information on a semipublic forum, we open the door for another company to claim ownership of the information. I also note that various formal agreements with multiple business partners explicitly forbid us from disclosing many kinds of business information. Given those agreements, who precisely is responsible for reviewing content posted on the social media platform?

As I offer these incredibly reasonable explanations, I realize that I'm acting the role of Dr. No. Instead of being a "team player," I'm the grumpy guy from the dreaded Office of No. What a predicament! But wait, it gets worse.

People stop me in the hallway or in the parking lot and ask me why we aren't using Skype. I explain to them that even though it's free, Skype has instant messaging capabilities. Publicly held companies are required by law to archive the messages sent and received by their employees. If for some reason in the future, a government agency or court of law requires a company to turn over logs of its instant messages, generating those logs can cost hundreds of thousands of dollars.

From my perspective as the CIO, anything that could potentially cost the company hundreds of thousands of dollars isn't free.

People also ask me about free services for storing and sharing files and documents. I have similar reservations about many of these free services. Some of them have already had security breaches. If a company's private documents suddenly become public, the damage would be costly. To me, that kind of risk isn't worth taking.

As a group, CIOs tend to be hyperaware of the potential security risks posed by some of the newer technologies. We're constantly reading about the latest cyber crimes, the most recent computer viruses, and the most nefarious hackers. As CIOs, we live in a different world—a world in which technology is both a blessing and a curse. We perceive the dangers, and the last thing we want is for something bad to happen on our watch.

Technology Is Not the Only Solution

I recently spoke with a CEO about the difference between the CIO and the company's other senior-level executives. Here's a brief summary of what he said to me:

> CIOs believe that most of the world's problems can be solved with technology. It's not surprising that you sincerely believe that. You went to college and you studied technology. Your

career and your success are based largely on understanding how technology works. You tend to see technology as the solution.

CEOs don't see the world that way. We see lots of possible solutions. Some of those solutions involve technology, but most of them involve something else, such as product development, finance, manufacturing, sales, marketing, distribution, customer service, or human resources.

It's hard for you to see the world through our eyes because you think that technology is always the right answer. It's the old story: If you've got a hammer, everything around you looks like a nail.

I agree that in today's modern economy, many problems can be solved by technology. But solving the most difficult problems usually requires a mix of several strategies. Technology is rarely the only solution or even the most desirable solution. CIOs tend to assume that every problem is reducible. Sometimes that just isn't the case. Sometimes you have to go with the best possible solution, and trust the people around you to make it work. That's what leadership is about—getting people aligned and working together to solve problems.

He is right, of course. CIOs *do* tend to overemphasize the problem-solving capabilities of technology. If I'm in a meeting of senior-level executives and someone mentions a problem, my first thought usually involves a technology-based solution. That's how I'm wired.

For years, CIOs struggled to get a "seat at the table" when company strategy was discussed. Many CIOs have earned that seat, and they are included regularly in top-level executive meetings.

Now that CIOs have higher profiles, however, more is expected of us. We need a broader, deeper portfolio of skills. The "hard" skills that brought us to our current posts must be augmented with "softer" skills that are typically associated with higher levels of management.

The View from the Crow's Nest

A friend recently told me a great story that illustrates the unique value that IT can bring to the enterprise. He's the CIO at a company that manufactures and markets industrial equipment. He asked me not to use his name or the name of the company. The story goes like this:

> The company's sales and manufacturing operations reported to different executives. In effect, they operated as independent units. There was no way for information to move horizontally from the sales force to the manufacturing division. The only points of contact between the two operations were at the senior management level, when the company's top executives would meet.
>
> Despite the company's best efforts, inventory was piling up at the company's warehouses. Nobody could figure out why. Then the CIO noticed something. He saw that the sales team was sending orders to the manufacturing division weeks and sometimes months before the deals themselves were finalized.
>
> After poking around, the CIO discovered that the sales team had developed a habit of ordering products before deals closed to avoid potential delays in delivery. As a sales rep told him, "We like to get a jump on things so our customers never have to wait too long for delivery after the deal is signed."
>
> From the perspective of the sales force, that made sense. Faster deliveries probably translated into happier customers and more repeat sales. But from the perspective of the rest of the company, the habit of placing orders long before deals were finalized made no sense. In fact, it was harming the company.
>
> The problem wasn't that one or two sales reps were placing orders for products that hadn't been formally sold— almost all of the sales reps had picked up the habit and were placing orders for products before deals were finalized and

checks cut. Naturally, some of those deals fell through or were delayed or modified. But the manufacturing division kept its end of the bargain, and produced whatever was ordered by the sales force.

You can imagine what happened. Instead of having one or two unsold orders sitting in warehouses, there were dozens of unsold orders sitting in warehouses. The CIO, who could see activity reports from all of the company's various divisions and operating units, figured out what was happening and alerted his boss, the CFO, who alerted the rest of the senior management team.

As a result, new processes were put in place to make sure that orders weren't produced until the deals were signed. The VP of sales and the VP of manufacturing met regularly to make sure that orders were produced and delivered as rapidly as possible.

The company might still be in the dark about its problem if the CIO hadn't proactively taken matters into his own hands. He read the reports, he noticed that something looked wrong, he took action to find out what was going on, and he alerted his boss as soon as he had figured out the cause of the problem.

I love this story because it really shows how IT can leverage its unique view across multiple units and silos to create real and lasting value for the company. CIOs and their IT departments can almost "feel" the heartbeat of a company. Like good doctors and nurses, they can tell when something is wrong and they know how to fix it.

The modern CIO has a virtually unobstructed view of the entire company. Smart companies recognize that and encourage their IT departments to act proactively when they see something that requires attention.

Unintentionally, but for all the right reasons, my friend transformed his company's IT department into the Office of Know.

Faster, Nimbler, and More Proactive

Filippo Passerini is president of Global Business Services and chief information officer at Procter & Gamble. When I visited P&G last year, I was impressed by the way in which IT contributed to the company's data-driven decision-making processes.

During my visit to P&G, Filippo recounted a senior-level meeting at which IT played a substantive role. When one of the executives asked a question about a particular business metric, referred to a report, or mentioned the results of a quantitative analysis performed within the company, an IT representative attending the meeting would quickly find the relevant data or information and present it to the executives on a large display screen. From my perspective, the meeting was a prime example of IT serving an important role as the Office of Know.

I spoke by phone recently with Filippo about the evolving responsibilities of the CIO in highly competitive organizations like P&G. Here are edited excerpts from our conversation:

> It is important to understand that IT has two critical dimensions. The first is providing operations infrastructure. I would categorize that as commodity work, something that must be managed for cost and productivity. The second dimension is building capabilities. That is what you saw at the meeting you attended. Seen from that viewpoint, there is no better time than now for the IT professional to play a leadership role in the business.
>
> But that means that the IT professional must fully understand the needs of the business and understand the business mind-set. Now the role is not focusing solely on cost and the usual concerns of operational management. Now the role is focusing on creating value and transformative innovation for the business.
>
> Remember that everything starts with transforming the business. The first question you have to ask is, "What are the

business benefits I expect? What is best for the business?" In the case of business analytics, for example, you need to ask, "What kind of analytics and what kind of models do I need to put in place to create the results that I want to deliver to the business?" Asking yourself those questions will guide you to the right analytics and the right models. Because if you just start giving a lot of analytical tools to everyone, without having done your own analysis first, things can get chaotic and dysfunctional pretty fast, despite your best intentions.

The best way to make sure that IT is delivering value is by giving people clear reasons and a clear strategy for the new technology you are providing. You need to marry what is needed with what is possible. At the same time, IT cannot wait for the business to make a request for new technology. IT should be proactive, and offer practical ideas to the business.

The real question is, "How do we create value fast?" In IT, we need the ability to divide large projects into stages, so we start delivering value sooner rather than later. The traditional way of doing an IT project—planning for six months and then taking two to three years before rolling it out—will not work anymore. Today you have to move at the pace of innovation, which is accelerating dramatically.

I like how Filippo captures the new spirit of IT leadership. I believe that his insight is spot on: In modern competitive markets, IT needs to focus on creating real value for the business, quickly and effectively.

Walking the Assembly Line

Here's another example of how IT's unique ability to see entire process-es from end to end can help the company. This story took place when I was an IT executive at the Ford Motor Company.

One of our plants was having a problem achieving full capacity. In automotive terms, capacity is measured in jobs per hour. At that time, full capacity was considered about sixty jobs per hour. In other words, an automobile rolls off the assembly line every minute.

This particular plant built trucks and cars. To avoid congestion at the end of the assembly process, the cars and trucks were built in alternating order—one car, followed by one truck, followed by one car, etc.

As I mentioned, this plant wasn't working to full capacity. Oddly, everyone there seemed to know exactly why: An enormous welding machine that was vital to the assembly process had to move back and forth every time that a new vehicle arrived for welding. It moved to accommodate the size differences between cars and trucks. Since the plant produced cars and trucks in alternating order, the welding machine spent a lot of time moving back and forth. As a result, the assembly process was delayed practically every time that a vehicle arrived at the welding station.

A similarly bizarre situation was occurring during the paint application stage. Cars and trucks were temporarily stored and then returned to the assembly line to be painted in the proper order. Again, the main concern seemed to be avoiding confusion and congestion at the final stages of the assembly process. But pulling the cars off the line and putting them back again took time. By the end of each shift, the lost seconds and lost minutes were really adding up. The result was lost productivity.

At each stage of the assembly process, the workers saw the problem as something caused at the stage immediately before the car or truck reached their station. They couldn't visualize the entire process.

Since most of the assembly processes were guided by software, I saw the situation differently. To me, it was a software problem that could be fixed relatively easily.

We wrote new software code that enabled us to weld six cars, followed by six trucks, without messing up the final stages of the process. Instead of moving back and forth every 60 seconds, the giant welding machine only had to move every six minutes. In addition to saving time, the welding machine now broke down less often and required fewer repairs.

It cost us about $10,000 to write the new software code. The resulting increase in efficiency saved us about $100,000 per hour.

As you can imagine, those kinds of numbers are greatly appreciated by top management.

All of this took place over a very brief span of time. The alternative solution was buying a second welding machine, which would have cost millions and taken months to install. The solution we devised cost thousands and took days.

I could visualize the solution because I could see the entire process from an IT perspective, and I knew instinctively that writing new software code would be less costly than buying another welding machine.

Gone Hunting

Another story from my time at Ford: We had an attendance problem at one of our plants. People worked hard and they wanted the company to succeed. But they also felt that after a particularly difficult shift or especially stressful week, they deserved some time off. And so they would call in sick. In Michigan, many of the workers were avid hunters. They would spend a day or two hunting, and then return to the plant relaxed and ready for work.

Since they were hourly workers and didn't get paid for hours they didn't work, they honestly felt that skipping work occasionally wasn't a big deal. I could see their point and I even agreed with them on a purely philosophical level. But I also knew that their absenteeism was costing the company money that we just couldn't afford to lose.

So I sat down with my team and had them write a computer program that kept track of the cost of absenteeism, including factors such as pension, healthcare, and other benefits that Ford had to pay whether the workers showed up or not. The program also tracked problems that arose when substitute workers were brought in. As expected, the substitutes made more mistakes, their stations accounted for more delays, and the overall quality of their work just wasn't as good as the regular workers.

I passed the information that we collected back to the managers, and they shared it with the workers. The information was highly granular and showed specifically how the quality and productivity at the plant suffered when experienced workers decided not to show up.

When the workers saw the information, they were shocked. They took genuine pride in the quality of their work, and there was a true spirit of competition among the various teams at the plant. They saw that when they took a day off to go hunting, there was a real impact. It hurt their team, the plant, the company, and the consumers who bought the cars we made.

After the workers digested the information and understood the downside of their behavior, attendance went up. They wanted to do a good job, and they didn't want the company to fail. Collectively, they made the right decision.

Moving from No to Yes

Let's return to the question of whether it's possible for the CIO to change his or her stripes and become less risk averse.

My straightforward answer is no. A competent CIO will never shed his or her natural desire to protect the company's IT assets. I believe that those guardian instincts are indeed hardwired into most CIOs.

What can change, however, is the unfortunate habit of top management to pass risks along to the IT department. When a CEO tells the CIO that "IT should just take care of that," what the CIO hears is that the risk is now on IT's shoulders, and if something goes wrong, IT will be blamed.

What the CIO needs to hear is something more like this: *Tell us what it will cost to implement Project X in a way that balances risks and rewards reasonably. Tell us if you don't have the money in the IT budget to fund Project X. If you don't have the funds in your budget, then senior management will decide whether to allocate additional funds, cancel an existing project, or cancel Project X.*

That kind of message sends a clear signal that top management has bought into the idea of sharing the risks and responsibilities of making a potentially difficult decision about an IT project. Now the CIO can relax a little. IT can become less fearful and more helpful. Dr. No becomes Dr. Yes, and the Office of No is transformed into the Office of Know.

Here's the important takeaway: IT doesn't hold the key to that transformation. The key is held by top management. If you—the CEO, the CFO, or the COO—are willing to share some of the CIO's pain, the CIO will gladly step up and do whatever is necessary to get the job done. As a CIO, I know that to be true. It's how we're wired.

CIOs tend to think like engineers. We're not fighter pilots. We can help you design the systems you need and we can keep them running. We are delighted to offer our expertise and happy to work tirelessly in a field that we truly love. All we ask in return is that you share a portion of the risk, understand the costs, and accept some of the responsibility of making decisions about which projects go forward, which are delayed, and which are scrapped.

My advice to CEOs, CFOs, and COOs is this:

1. Use the CIO as your "eyes and ears."
2. Trust the CIO to act on your behalf.
3. Share the risk and understand the true costs of IT.

If you take that advice, I personally guarantee that you will get higher returns from your IT investments.

QUESTIONS THE C-SUITE NEEDS TO ASK

1. Does your organization see IT as an asset or a cost? If IT is perceived as a cost, what would it take to turn it into an asset?

2. Is the CIO perceived as a trusted source of valuable information and expertise?

3. Is the organization leveraging the talent and expertise of its IT team? Does the organization see IT as integral to its overall success in the market?

CHAPTER 9

Enterprise
Resource Planning

One Size Fits Most

EXECUTIVE SUMMARY

ERP systems require enormous investments of time and money, but the rationale for ERP implementations is often misunderstood. When such large sums of money are at stake, it is absolutely critical for executives to fully understand the pros and cons of ERP systems, as well as the available alternatives.

ERP Basics

Any discussion about IT systems would be incomplete without a corresponding discussion of Enterprise Resource Planning (ERP) software. ERP systems are important because they support the entire business. The precursors of ERP systems were Manufacturing Resource Planning (MRP) systems. MRP systems arose from the need to manage manufacturing facilities and improve the alignment between financial, purchasing, and the plant floor scheduling systems. ERP systems are the next evolutionary step beyond MRP systems. In addition to connecting more systems than MRP implementations, ERP systems were designed to address a growing awareness that data from one part of the enterprise can be useful in other parts of the enterprise.

Modern ERP systems encompass nearly every area of the enterprise and often include wide-ranging functions such as customer relationship management (CRM), human resources (HR), and supply chain resource management. Suffice it to say that since ERP systems were introduced two decades ago, their scope has broadened dramatically.

The two biggest players in the enterprise software business are Oracle and SAP, which dominate the high end of the market. There are also many ERP vendors that cater primarily to small and medium-sized businesses. The main strength of ERP systems—their ability to perform just about every imaginable task—is also a weakness, since ERP systems rarely perform any single task exceptionally well.

ERP versus Best of Breed

One of the challenges companies have when they look at ERP systems is figuring out whether it makes more sense to have one system that does everything pretty well instead of having many individual systems that perform separate tasks exceedingly well. Over the long term, ERP is probably more efficient and more cost-effective than the alternative strategy, which is usually referred to as *best of breed*. The advantage of the best of breed approach is that it lets you choose the best solution for each business situation you face. The disadvantage of best of breed is that it becomes very expensive to connect, maintain, and upgrade all of those disparate systems. That is why it is very important for executives to understand the difference between ERP systems and best of breed systems.

When I explain the difference between ERP and best of breed, I use the analogy of buying shoes for everyone in the company. Imagine that you want to buy really great shoes for everyone, but that the shoes you want only come in size 10. For most people, the shoes will be fine. For many people, a little adjustment will be required. But for lots of other people, the shoes will be simply too large or too small.

Many companies use ERP systems and find them a good fit. But there are also companies that just cannot use them. Naturally, the vendors will tell you that with a little adjustment, their systems will work just fine. As an executive, however, you need to determine whether ERP is a good fit or not.

When considering ERP systems, remember that one size fits most but not all companies. The problem with "one size fits most" is that many companies are bound to suffer expensive disappointments.

It is also important to remember that when a vendor says that an ERP system can be modified to fit your specific needs, what the vendor really means is that anything is possible with a sufficient amount of customization. Keep in mind that the customization will be expensive and that it will likely increase your switching costs in the future.

Single Instance versus Multiple Systems

Choosing between ERP and best of breed involves asking questions and considering tradeoffs. ERP offers many benefits, but not every set of users will experience the benefits in the same way. And some users will undoubtedly wish for the return of "the good old days," when each department had its own IT system.

A single ERP system is likely to offer more efficiencies than multiple systems. But some of those older systems offered specific advantages that would be difficult to replicate in an ERP system. Again, it is important for executives to weigh the efficiencies and convenience of an ERP system against the "comfort" provided by a legacy system. It can be a hard choice, but it is a choice that has to be made and then clearly explained so that people don't feel as though their needs or desires are being ignored.

Some companies leave the choice to individual business units. That introduces an element of flexibility and creates options that might lead to greater efficiencies in the future. For most organizations, there is no "right" or "wrong" answer—you have to make the best possible choice for your business.

There is a lot to be said for keeping things flexible. The trend today is for companies to standardize enterprise-wide functions such as accounting and human resources and let individual operating units pick systems that address their specific needs.

Keeping ERP Systems Up to Date

ERP systems need to be updated and upgraded on a regular basis. On average, ERP vendors release new versions of their systems every five to six years. In the same way that you need to upgrade your PC's operating system, you need to upgrade your ERP system. The difference is that ERP systems are a lot more complex than PCs. Instead of simply installing a new version of Windows and familiarizing yourself with the quirks of the new version, you have to upgrade an enterprise-level system and retrain thousands of users. Sometimes, a new upgrade will undo some or all of the custom configurations you created to make the system more business friendly. Now you have to recustomize and reconfigure the upgraded system. That additional work can take years. It can also get very expensive.

ERP upgrades can easily consume huge chunks of your IT budget. If you have multiple versions or systems for various operating units, your costs can escalate dramatically. For example, if you have 27 business units and they all have their own versions of the corporate system, then you have to do 27 upgrades of 27 different systems. That's why some companies insist on implementing a global, single-instance ERP system—you do one upgrade for the entire company, and that's it.

There's also an advantage in terms of hardware. A global single instance is basically one very large computer system. As you can imagine, buying one computer system is less expensive than buying 27 computer systems. It's not exactly 1/27th of the cost, because a global single-instance system has to be significantly larger and faster, but there are some significant economies of scale compared to having multiple smaller systems.

As you can see, there are plenty of factors that need to be thoroughly examined and understood before making a decision. Based on my own experiences, I can tell you that there are no perfect solutions. Each choice involves challenges and tradeoffs. Ideally, the choices you make will have a net positive impact on the business.

Generally speaking, a highly diversified business with multiple operating units in many parts of the world might not benefit greatly from a global single instance system. On the other hand, if your enterprise is already highly standardized and your operating units are virtually carbon copies of each other, then go for a global single instance.

Intel, for example, has standardized its factories; each is exactly the same, down to the number of steps you take to reach a certain part of the building or a particular room. I am not familiar with Intel's ERP system, but I would guess that it is a single-instance system.

Again, there is neither a right nor a wrong answer. A global single-instance system will probably bring down costs, but there will be less flexibility and it might take longer for the company to respond to changes in the market. You get a great shoe, but it only comes in one size.

Taking a best of breed approach will almost certainly be more expensive, but it will enable the company to respond more quickly to changes in the outside world. It will also require a larger IT organization to keep all the various parts and systems working together smoothly, and (as mentioned earlier) upgrades will be particularly challenging.

That being said, choosing an ERP system does not render you immune to the pain of upgrading. Because ERP systems often take years to install, it is not uncommon for upgrades to be released before a system goes live. That means that you have to delay going live until the system is upgraded, which can add months or years to the implementation. That is the painful reality of ERP systems.

QUESTIONS THE C-SUITE NEEDS TO ASK

1. How comfortable are you with the idea of a "one size fits most" ERP system?

2. Have you already standardized most of your key business processes?

3. Are you comfortable with the idea of a long implementation timeframe and the potential for many delays for the ERP system goes live?

CHAPTER **10**

Outsourcing IT

EXECUTIVE SUMMARY

Since it's highly unlikely that the IT organization has access to all the resources it needs within its own four walls, most CIOs rely to various degrees on outsourcing. It's important to see outsourcing as a standard part of your business strategy and to devote the time and energy required to getting it right.

Three Strategies

IT outsourcing is definitely not a one-size-fits-all proposition. Your IT outsourcing strategy should be aligned with the overall business strategy of the company, and it must directly serve the company's specific business goals.

In this chapter, we will look at three distinct types of IT outsourcing:

1. Wholesale
2. Targeted
3. Outcome-based

I've had plenty of experience with all three kinds. Some of my experiences with outsourcing have been positive, and some have been negative. All of those experiences were instructive, and I hope that you will find them valuable.

In 1985, I interviewed with General Motors and was hired. The Monday that I was scheduled to report to work, I was informed that I was not, in fact, to be working for GM, but would instead be an employee of EDS (Electronic Data Systems). That was my first experience with wholesale outsourcing. GM had outsourced its IT operations (and most of its IT staff, including me) to EDS, the company launched by Ross Perot.

I was sent a copy of the bestselling book *On Wings of Eagles*, which recounts the 1978 rescue of two EDS executives who had been arrested in Tehran. Additionally, I was told that I had to wear a suit, since that was the dress code at EDS. (At GM, it was okay for managers to wear sports jackets.)

At that particular time, EDS was a wholly-owned subsidiary of GM, and the general feeling was that if something was good for EDS, it was also good for GM. As you can imagine, that philosophy made it difficult for GM to manage its IT costs. One particularly memorable example of this was GM's decision to buy PCs priced at $8,000 per unit. The prevailing sentiment was, "We own EDS, so why does it matter?"

In retrospect, I call this approach to wholesale outsourcing a *capitulation strategy*, because you are surrendering your control of IT and hoping for a good outcome. Basically, you're throwing up your hands, saying, "I can't deal with this," and sweeping your IT problem under the carpet. It rarely works. You can't make problems go away by outsourcing them—in fact, outsourcing problems often makes them worse because you no longer feel a direct obligation to solve them. For many managers, outsourcing means someone else can be blamed if something goes wrong.

That being said, there's nothing intrinsically wrong with outsourcing IT. There is something intrinsically wrong, though, with outsourcing a problem. When you have a problem, it's your responsibility to solve it.

In some situations, however, wholesale outsourcing can be an acceptable solution. For example, when I was at Ford, we spun off our parts group, Visteon, into a separate company. At Ford, we knew exactly what we were spending to provide Visteon with the IT services it required. Since Visteon needed to ramp up its operations quickly after the spinoff, it made sense to outsource most of its IT needs to a group of vendors.

But even that arrangement had a limited shelf-life. Over the course of several years, the outsourcers failed to keep up with advances in technology that would have allowed for much greater efficiency, and as a result, Visteon did not take advantage of new technologies that could have reduced its IT costs.

The experience taught me a valuable lesson: Do not assume that your outsourcing vendors will stay abreast of the latest developments in technology. In truth, Visteon's outsourcing vendors had little incentive to upgrade their technology. The other important lesson I learned from the Visteon experience is always make sure that technology upgrades are included in your outsourcing contracts.

Your Vendor Is Not Your Partner

Much has been written about the importance of partnerships between IT vendors and their customers. In 2007, my good friend Mike Barlow co-authored a book titled *Partnering with the CIO*, in which he explains why IT vendors should focus on establishing long-term strategic relationships with key customers.

The idea of partnering with the CIO is a great idea—if you are a vendor. It's not such a great idea if you're a customer. In fact, partnering with IT vendors can be downright dangerous to the financial health of your company.

The Visteon experience illustrates the problems that can arise when customers start thinking about vendors as their partners. In the Visteon example, the reason that the outsourcing vendors did not stay abreast of newer and more cost-effective technologies was simple: It was not in their financial interests to upgrade their existing technologies. Their goal was increasing profits. If they could deliver the contracted service levels with older and less efficient equipment, there was no incentive for them to upgrade. From my perspective, that's not a partnership.

I'm not saying that you should be mean or unfriendly to vendors. But please don't treat them as partners. Their job is minimizing their costs and maximizing their profits. They do not share your goals and they do not always have your best interests in mind. In truth, the goals of IT service vendors can be very much at odds with the goals of your business. Once you accept that as fact, it's easier to focus on arranging deals that make sense for your company.

When I talk to vendors I tell them straightforwardly that we are not partners. We can have a great business relationship that lasts over many years and generates many benefits for both sides. But our basic interests will remain at odds. My interest is getting the most service at the lowest price. Their interest is maximizing the profit of any deal they make.

I also make it a practice to have at least two vendors for every important service or project that we outsource. When you have two vendors, they must compete with each other; they are less likely to seek the quickest profit because each vendor knows there's a competitor waiting in the wings to take a larger chunk of the deal.

In my experience, the typical vendor will assign its best people to work with you at the beginning of an engagement and then replace them over time with less experienced and less expensive people. From the vendor's perspective, that practice makes perfect sense. But from my perspective, it means I'm getting less value from the engagement. Creating a competitive environment makes that practice somewhat less likely.

Managing two vendors requires more work on my part, but I've found that the extra work is worth the effort.

The Value of Being Selective

Not long after I was hired as CIO at Terex, the company embarked on a strategic transformation. Terex went from being a holding company to an operating company. For IT, the company's transformation meant a whole new set of duties and responsibilities. As the company's CIO, I could have pushed for a wholesale outsourcing arrangement with a major IT services vendor.

My experiences at Ford and General Motors had taught me valuable lessons about outsourcing, and I firmly believed that a wholesale IT outsourcing arrangement would have represented a total capitulation. At the same time, I knew that we had to get a bunch of systems up and running very quickly. So I developed a highly selective outsourcing strategy in which we would keep some IT responsibilities in-house and outsource others to vendors.

The first step in developing a targeted outsourcing strategy involved making a thorough inventory of IT responsibilities and then deciding which of those responsibilities could and should be managed internally.

Some of the decisions were based on cost and some based on other factors. For example, we could have set up our own corporate e-mail systems for less money than it would have cost to outsource it, but the process of setting it up would have been a distraction. So we decided to outsource our e-mail system, even though we could have done it more cheaply ourselves.

I made a similar decision about our help desk. We could have outsourced it and saved some money, but we had a lot of capability in-house and I had a hunch that we could do a better job than an outside vendor.

Obviously, we didn't want to outsource the migration of systems that handled confidential financial information or sensitive customer information. As a result, we handled our ERP implementation in-house, but we outsourced the computer systems that ran the ERP software. We decided to outsource our data center operations because we didn't have a data center and we didn't have the time to hire the people we would need to build it and run it, such as database infrastructure architects and DBAs (database analysts).

Our targeted outsourcing strategy also gave us an advantage when dealing with vendors, since they knew we were basing our decisions on multiple criteria. Frankly, we were able to get better deals than we would have gotten if we had opted for wholesale outsourcing, or painted ourselves into a corner by insisting on the fastest implementation at the lowest possible cost.

Targeted outsourcing enabled us to get the best vendor deals without sacrificing the levels of quality and flexibility required by our business units to compete successfully in their markets.

Outsourcing to the Cloud

From my perspective, the cloud is a platform for commoditization. The advantage of cloud-based IT services is speed—you can move much more quickly when you're in the cloud because the infrastructure and the applications are already there. You just have to decide how much you want.

The problem with the cloud, again from my perspective, is that it can be another way to move problems around without solving them. Outsourcing a problem to the cloud doesn't make the problem go away; it just shifts the problem to another location.

In many respects, I view the cloud as an alternative billing model. As a customer, you don't have to physically purchase the hardware and the applications, but you certainly do have to pay for them. All the cloud vendor has done is to make some aspects of the problem that you're trying to solve seem simpler. If simplicity is your only goal, then the cloud can be a good choice. But you will pay for that simplicity.

After all, why do you think that vendors are jumping into the cloud? They're jumping into the cloud because selling cloud-based services is more profitable than selling just hardware and software. They're not doing you any favors. For vendors, the cloud is a lucrative business model, a way to make money.

For example, we recently looked at buying a solution for managing CAD (computer-aided design) data. We sketched out a five-year budget, and the general feeling of the executive team was that it would be too expensive. Then someone asked how much it would cost to manage the CAD data in a cloud-based model. The answer was $100 per month, per engineer. The executive team seemed pleased, until the CEO pulled out his calculator and did the math. It turned out that buying the solution would cost the same as "renting" the solution from a cloud vendor.

Cloud vendors love to talk about how their operating models allow you to "pay by the drink" for IT service. I think that most of us would agree that if you can afford to buy the whole bottle, it doesn't make sense to buy drinks separately.

In my judgment, the cloud only *seems* less expensive than traditional IT. For example, Salesforce.com is unquestionably one of the most popular and successful providers of cloud-based services. If you are a small company with two or three sales reps Salesforce is a great deal. The product is wonderful and the barrier to entry is low. But if you are a large company, with 2,000 or 3,000 sales reps, then Salesforce maybe isn't such a great deal. For the small company, the monthly cost of using Salesforce will be a couple of hundred dollars. But for the large company, the monthly cost of using Salesforce can run into hundreds of thousands of dollars—which is great for Salesforce but probably not so great for you. If you have thousands of sales reps, then a traditional CRM system might make more financial sense than a cloud service.

Additionally, larger companies have the scale and the resources to build or buy systems that meet their specific needs more closely than cloud solutions. Traditional vendors will hand-tailor solutions for you because the cost of customization is already baked into their business models. Most cloud vendors can offer only limited customization, because their business models depend on providing the same basic products and services to all customers.

Scale Counts

Here's a story that illustrates how scale counts when you're trying to determine whether to build, buy, or rent IT. The story takes place when I was at Ford. We were looking at mobile systems for monitoring the maintenance status of our manufacturing machines. We found a vendor that made software that ran on handheld monitoring devices. The software for each device cost $750.

If you are a small company with one factory and a handful of machines, then spending $750 per device for software makes perfect sense. But at Ford, we didn't need just one of the devices—we needed thousands. I went back to my office and figured out that it would cost us about $50,000 to write a program that would run on handheld monitoring devices.

I told the vendor that we would be happy to pay $50,000 for 1,000 copies of its software. The vendor said the discount I was seeking was too steep and refused my offer. From the vendor's perspective, the value of the deal was $750,000 ($750 per device x 1,000). From my perspective, however, the value of the software was $50,000.

It was relatively easy for me to obtain the approvals necessary to spend $50,000, especially after I explained that writing the software ourselves would save us roughly $700,000.

But it's easy to imagine a similar scenario taking place at a smaller company, where buying software for $750 per device would make a lot more sense than developing the software from scratch.

My experience with the handheld monitoring solution definitely influenced my views on cloud-based IT services. In small quantities, the cloud makes sense. If you are a small or medium-sized company, the cloud offers speed and a low entry barrier.

I know CIOs at large companies who have brought in Salesforce in the belief that only a handful of people would use it. But here's what generally happens: The five people using Salesforce tell all of their colleagues and before you know it, you have hundreds and then thousands of people using Salesforce.

Again, that's all good news for Salesforce, and it speaks volumes about the quality of the company's products. But it's not good news for the company using Salesforce, because suddenly their "little experiment" in the cloud has escalated into a huge cost.

For large companies, the best course of action is comparing costs on the basis of apples to apples and oranges to oranges. In other words, don't be misled by the low entry costs of outsourcing IT to the cloud. If you aren't careful and if you don't do your homework, your costs can expand tremendously.

Offshoring

Offshoring of IT services became a common phenomenon in the late 1990s and the early years of the 21st century. The basic idea was taking advantage of wage differences between skilled IT workers in the United States and skilled IT workers in less economically developed nations, such as India. U.S. companies also outsourced IT operations to Poland, Ireland, and Hungary. I think it's fair to say that for a period of roughly ten years, any country with an educated workforce and low wages became a potential destination for offshoring.

Initially, offshoring offered tremendous advantages. When IT workers were earning $70 per hour in the United States and $12 per hour in India, it wasn't difficult to make the case for offshoring IT services.

In recent years, however, the advantages of offshoring have clearly diminished. IT workers in India now earn $30 to $40 per hour, and because of the generally weak economy, many IT workers in the United States are willing to accept lower wages than in the past.

On a recent trip to Michigan, I saw billboards urging businesses to "offshore to Detroit." From my perspective, domestic offshoring makes sense when you consider the downsides commonly associated with traditional offshoring, such as language issues, time zone differences, the near impossibility of assembling teams for face-to-face meetings, and myriad logistical challenges.

Earlier, I mentioned my practice of having two vendors for every significant outsourcing project. That practice is especially important when dealing with offshore vendors. You need a reliable mechanism for making sure that they're always giving you their best possible effort. Based on my experience, setting up a competitive scenario is the best way to sustain the highest levels of performance from vendors, no matter where they are located.

Outcome-Based Outsourcing

Outcome-based outsourcing has been around for a while, but it was typically applied in limited circumstances. Recently, outcome-based deals have been applied in a wider variety of IT scenarios, and that's why it's important for the C-suite to understand the benefits and trade-offs of outcome-based arrangements.

Here's a generic example of a traditional outcome-based deal: A vendor offers to help you lower your telecommunications costs. In return for lowering your costs by 25 percent annually, the vendor gets to keep one-third of the savings. The deal is attractive because you don't have to pay upfront—the vendor only makes money when it reduces your costs. The deal is a win-win scenario; both sides of the arrangement benefit. As a CIO, those types of deals are particularly attractive because the vendor assumes the risk—if the vendor can't find ways to save you money, the vendor doesn't earn a profit.

Some of the larger vendors are applying outcome-based outsourcing models more generally across the IT services portfolio. At the risk of contradicting myself, some of the outcome-based deals I'm hearing about almost seem like partnerships, in the sense that both parties are aligned and share similar goals.

For example, let's say that you're building a new e-commerce system and you're looking for a vendor to develop the system's shopping cart capability. In the past, you would have paid a vendor a fee for developing the project. Today, you might consider offering the vendor a percentage of the additional revenue generated by the new shopping cart feature. And you would tie payment to the achievement of your business goals. If one of your goals is increasing sales by 5 percent, you might offer the vendor 50 percent of your profits over 3 percent for 12 months.

That type of arrangement incents the vendor to deliver a viable product *and* stay focused on the tangible business results that your company has set out to achieve. Although outcome-based deals might seem like common sense, they represent a very different approach to doing business, both for the vendor and the customer.

Here's another generic example of an outcome-based outsourcing deal: Let's say that you're planning to reduce your inventory of physical servers through virtualization. In the past, you probably would have bought virtualization software and handled the project in-house. Today, you might seek an outcome-based deal in which a vendor handles the migration from physical to virtual servers. In return, the vendor keeps 30 percent of your cost savings.

As you can imagine, there are many ways to arrange an outcome-based outsourcing deal. The key is making sure that both you and the vendor benefit from achieving a successful outcome.

It seems likely that large vendors will take the lead in promoting outcome-based outsourcing and applying it across a broad spectrum of industries. I recommend keeping an eye on these deals as they are reported in industry publications and taking note of the details as they emerge.

Because outcome-based outsourcing is just beginning to catch on as a trend, don't expect people at your company to be experts—now is the time to explore, learn, and experiment. My hunch is that the trend will accelerate, and some variant of outcome-based outsourcing will eventually become the new norm.

Meantime, it's important to remember that many of the benefits generated by outsourcers also can be generated in-house. My advice is to look at any outsourcing deal you have and ask yourself if you could provide the same benefit with internal resources. Outsourcers aren't miracle workers or magicians; they're experts at cutting costs down to bare minimums. In my experience, there's nothing an outsourcer can do that you can't do yourself—if you're willing to make the effort.

QUESTIONS THE C-SUITE NEEDS TO ASK

1. How recently has the organization reviewed its outsourcing strategies?

2. Is outsourcing being used to create real advantages in the market, or merely to shift problems?

3. Do all C-level executives understand the risks and rewards associated with the three main types of outsourcing (wholesale, targeted, outcome-based)?

CHAPTER **11**

Rebaselining the
IT Budget

EXECUTIVE SUMMARY

Funding issues, rather than technology, are often the main drivers of IT project failures. When a project runs out of money, it's important for the CIO to have a range of practical fallbacks or workarounds. Poor decisions made in a panic can exacerbate the situation.

Robbing Peter to Pay Paul Is Not a Good Business Strategy

When IT projects fail, or when they underperform relative to expectations, it's often due to lack of sufficient funding. Over the course of my career, I've noticed that underfunding generally occurs for one of two reasons:

1. The project is underfunded initially.
2. The project becomes underfunded over time.

This chapter deals mostly with the second reason, and offers a fairly straightforward solution.

Let's look at a typical IT budget scenario. We'll begin with the assumption that each project within the overall IT budget has its own budget. Most IT departments track overall spending over time. But it's also important to track spending on individual projects relative to the percent of the project's completion.

If you're not tracking spending relative to completion, then it's easy to wind up in a situation where you're on budget, but you're behind schedule. As the saying goes, "Time is money." Running out of time can have the same net effect as running out of money.

For example, let's say the business wants a new sales forecasting process and they come to IT in June with a project that could potentially take six months. IT follows its company's budget process to capture all the costs (hardware, software, people, etc.). Those costs are then compared to the value the project is expected to deliver.

If the project looks like it will deliver good value, the company will find a way to fund it. Different companies have different processes for allocating capital, but the end result is usually the same: A dollar amount is allocated over a certain period of time.

Let's say this particular project is budgeted at $600,000 over six months. If you start in June and finish in December, your rate of spending is $100,000 per month. As long as you stay within the project's monthly budget, everything looks fine—you're on budget.

But let's say the project takes two months longer to complete than you thought it would take, which can be a fairly common occurrence with IT projects. Now you're looking at being $200,000 over budget— even though your monthly spending for the project is on target.

I'm sure that you can see where all of this is leading: You assume, since your monthly spending is on target that your annual spending is on target, too. But as it turns out, that's not the case. Now you have painted yourself into a tight corner and your options are limited.

So what do you do? The most common—and wrong—response would be to find unspent money from somewhere else in the IT budget and use it to fund the rest of the project. Maybe you can find money in your capital budget, or maybe you can find money in your operating budget. Either way, you're robbing Peter to pay Paul, and that's not a good way to operate your IT department.

The Annual Budget Trap

Here's a better way to run IT: Rethink the idea of an annual budget. Most IT departments have annual budgets. Those budgets look great on paper, but they rarely cover the contingencies of modern business. Today's markets are continually shifting, changing, and transforming.

As the Marines say, "Expect the unexpected." Change is a constant, but the pace of change is accelerating. Soon, the idea of anything staying the same for more than thirty days will seem hopelessly old-fashioned. Given the astonishing pace of transformation today, does it really make sense to budget IT on an annual basis?

I think the answer is no, it does not make sense. Has there been a year in recent memory in which an unexpected change in the market and/or the introduction of a transformational technology has *not* occurred at some time during the year—after the IT budget has been set—and forced a midcourse correction in IT spending?

Let me rephrase the question: When was the last time that a major shift, in either the market or the technology landscape, occurred at the very moment *before* you began preparing next year's IT budget? That's never happened to me, I can assure you!

Here's a more likely scenario: Some unexpected change in the business landscape or tectonic shift in market dynamics takes place at the *least* opportune moment, at a time when the IT budget has already been signed, sealed, and delivered with every penny of spending accounted.

And that's basically why I don't believe that annual budgeting makes sense for IT. Budget processes are designed to help organizations, not hurt them. But when a company insists that IT stick to an annual budget, it actually increases the chances that something bad will happen.

For example, most IT budgets include capital expenses (capex) and operating expenses (opex). Now let's say there's a sudden change in the market and one of the company's business units needs to respond rapidly. The CIO will feel pressure to act swiftly on the business unit's request. But there's no money in the budget to cover whatever it is that the business needs at this particular moment. Faced with a dilemma, the average CIO will likely take money from the operating side of the budget to pay for the business unit's request—something that normally would be considered a capital expense.

As we all know, this kind of behavior happens frequently, but that doesn't make it right or even smart. In fact, when situations like these arise—and they do arise more often than anyone would prefer to admit—they tend to reinforce a set of bad behaviors that almost invariably lead to negative outcomes.

Let's say the CIO decides to play it safe and leave the opex budget untouched. Instead, the CIO looks at the capex budget and picks an existing project—a project that has already been approved and funded—to defund. Now we're right back to robbing Peter to pay Paul. Somebody in the company must have made a business case for the existing project, or it wouldn't have been included in the budget. That somebody—whoever he or she is—will certainly be disappointed when the CIO announces that the project has been scaled down, postponed, or outright canceled.

The remarkable thing about these types of scenarios is that they are not remarkable—they are, in fact, quite common. If you're the CIO and you're running IT with an annual budget, your options for coping with an unexpected request are extremely limited. And if you ask the CFO or the board for more money to cover the costs of implementing the request, the likely response will be, "Gee, we're already spending lots of money on IT, so you should figure out how to get it (whatever it is) done and stop asking us for more money."

And if you follow that advice, you will inevitably end up shortchanging another project. That's the reality of annual budgeting.

The other negative aspect of annual budgeting is that when you find yourself with unspent money, you feel an obligation to buy something. This often results in late-December shopping sprees for new servers or other equipment that you might or might not really need, but that you feel you should buy so it doesn't look as though you overestimated your annual spending requirements.

Does all of this seem a bit neurotic? Well, it should. It's more than neurotic—it's bad business, plain and simple. It leads to a vicious cycle of spending more than you need in some years and underfunding projects in other years. Let's take a pledge not to operate in this manner. Remember, we are stewards of the company's finances, and we have a fiduciary responsibility.

That being said, flexibility and speed are also essential to the health of the business. Market conditions constantly change, and unexpected requests are made. That's the reality we live in. It's important to judge projects on their value to the company, whether those projects surface at the beginning, middle, or end of the fiscal year. Yes, it would be convenient if your markets remained static over the course of your fiscal year. But that isn't likely to happen. Your markets will change, and the business will ask IT for new projects that aren't in the budget.

A Different Approach

Any company that wants to remain competitive will evaluate new IT projects throughout the year. Finding the money to pay for worthwhile projects shouldn't become a scavenger hunt.

Rebaselining the IT budget is an alternative. Here's how it works: Let's say you've got a $10 million capital budget for the year. Six months into the year, someone comes up with a brilliant project that will save the company $5 million annually. But the project will cost $2 million, and you've already spent or allocated every penny of your capital budget.

The old way to handle this problem would have been to take the money from another project or shift money from your operating budget. Both are bad choices that will likely yield negative results.

Here's a better option: Rebaseline the IT capex budget from $10 million to $12 million. Go back to the board, or to the CFO, or to the IT governance committee and explain the situation. Lay the choices out for them, show them the options, and offer a range of likely outcomes.

If the project will really save the company $10 million annually for several years, then it would be crazy not to fund it. And if the new project is going to save the company money, then why should the CIO be forced to reduce funding for an existing project? From my perspective, it makes a lot more sense to rebaseline the budget than it does to put an existing project at risk.

But let's say the company just doesn't have an additional $2 million to spend. What do you do now? The initial steps are the same: You go back to the board, the CFO, or the IT governance committee and you spell it out for them, in detail. You explain the choices and show them precisely what's most likely to happen if funding is shifted to the new project. You remind them that they have skin in the game—and that an existing project will be have to be scaled down or sacrificed.

It is easy for a CIO to assume the answer is to spend more money, but rebaselining should be applied to reductions as well. Markets might change, a new product introduction doesn't hit its targets, or other factors, are all times to look at IT costs like any other function and rebaseline. Maybe SLAs for helpdesk should be reduced, or new PCs should be delayed to offset other business conditions.

Maybe the final decision will be to delay the new project. But more likely the decision will be to table or postpone one or more of the existing projects. What's important is the way in which the decision is reached—it has to be a group effort. IT shouldn't be asked or required to "bite the bullet" or "take one for the team." That kind of thinking reflects an obsolete cultural bias that pits IT against "the business."

In today's enterprise, IT and the business are inseparable. What happens to the business impacts IT, and what happens to IT impacts the business.

Of course, you need to be prudent. And you need to remember that this isn't about rebaselining individual projects—it's about rebaselining IT budgets.

For example, let's say that you have $14 million capex budget. In that capex budget are four major projects, each budgeted at $3 million, and $2 million budgeted for miscellaneous projects.

You begin work on the four major projects. Three months into the year, the projects are progressing well, but they're not completed. Then someone has a brilliant idea for a new project that will enable the company to compete successfully in a new market and make lots of money.

If the cost of that new project is more than $2 million, you are in a tough spot. You will have to decide which of the four ongoing projects to cancel, postpone, or scale back. Making those decisions will be difficult, because you've already invested capital in each of the projects and because the people in the business who are counting on those projects to help them achieve their goals will be disappointed.

If you decide to cancel a project outright, you might be forced to write off the capital investment. That's generally considered a very big negative, but it's one of the choices that you have.

Or you can rebaseline the capex budget and track to that number going forward. Yes, that might involve getting approvals from various people, but the alternatives are worse. In my experience, I've found that people will do practically everything to avoid canceling a project, especially if it has popular support and senior-level sponsorship. As a result, projects tend to be delayed or pushed out, instead of outright canceled.

Here's the problem with delaying a project: It costs more to complete. You don't save money when you delay or extend a project—you make it more expensive! Sure, that might sound counterintuitive, but think about it for a minute: Time is money. The more hours it takes to finish a project, the more it's going to cost.

And that's not the worst part. The worst part is that you are also delaying the business benefits of whatever the delayed project was intended to deliver. Remember, you didn't just decide to do the project for no particular reason—there was a business case and an expected ROI. Someone expected a tangible, positive result (such as increased sales revenue or lower unit costs) from the project. And now that tangible result will be delayed.

Wait, it gets even worse. Chances are that when you're trying to figure out how to capitalize the new project, you will try to spread the pain by delaying or cutting back on all four of the ongoing projects. But your attempt to distribute the pain evenly only magnifies the problem by adding costs to all of the projects—while at the same time reducing their expected benefits.

So even though it might seem like you're saving money, you're actually wasting money and digging yourself into a deeper hole.

Moore's Law and the Cost of IT

One of the main reasons that IT is asked to "absorb" new costs is that they always seem to have a secret stash of money for these contingences. This is partially true. Gorden Moore postulated in 1965 that the number of integrated circuits on a board would double every two years.

What this means is that technology shrinks. What is not fully understood is that as technology shrinks manufacturing costs of technology shrink as well. Since many organizations, budgets are built on an assumption of last year's costs, there is usually a way to use less expensive technologies to reduce spend.

As the chips become less of the cost of technology (think about a $400 PC today with a CPU, wired and wireless card, case, power supply, keyboard/mouse, and disk drive; what percentage of the cost is the CPU versus 10 years ago?) it is more difficult to find savings but not impossible. I put a budget number in my objectives every year on "cost savings." Most years that is respent against new initiatives, but by calling it out separate you make it clear that each new project must be funded, either from the savings money or new capital. There is no secret stash to fund new initiatives.

And the Moral of the Story Is . . .

Don't try to spread your IT budget like peanut butter. Instead, look at each individual IT project on the basis of expected value. If the ROI looks good, go forward and make sure it's fully funded. If you suspect that the ROI won't live up to expectations, cancel the project.

But the key takeaway is this: IT should not be forced into making the decision in a vacuum. Senior management must participate in the decision for the simple reason that almost every IT decision affects every part of the enterprise. Sure, there will be a handful of IT projects that mostly impact the IT organization. But the overwhelming majority of IT projects exist to serve specific business needs and accomplish specific business objectives. Gone are the days when the business could say "just get it done" and leave the details for the CIO to sort out.

Before leaving this chapter, let's briefly touch on a related topic: aggregating cost. There's a tendency to look at the IT budget at its highest level of aggregated cost. In other words, rolling everything up into one big number that becomes "the IT budget."

That number might look great on a PowerPoint slide, but it's not going to help you manage IT spending in a modern enterprise that's coping with rapidly evolving markets and continually changing customer needs.

At best, the aggregate number is a blurry picture. You need to go down a couple of levels to understand the "mechanics" of your spending. You need to separate your capital costs and your operating costs, your hardware costs and your people costs, your one-time costs and your recurring costs. There are no shortcuts or alternatives to having a deep understanding of how IT works and what it costs, at every level.

The good news is that when you look closely at all of those levels, you will make better decisions. Imagine if the CFO decided to put all of the company's selling, general, and administrative expenses (SG&A) into one bucket and then said, "Our SG&A is too high; we have to reduce it." The results wouldn't be pretty, I can assure you.

The devil is in the details. Aggregate numbers might be fine for Wall Street analysts, but they're not especially helpful when you're a C-level executive trying to make critical decisions about spending that will impact the company's ability to succeed in competitive markets. You wouldn't aggregate your SG&A, so please resist the urge to aggregate your IT costs.

Some IT Projects Are Very Expensive

Most of this chapter has dealt with handling situations in which projects are initially funded at the right level, but then become underfunded over time. At the beginning of the chapter, I mentioned that some projects are underfunded initially, which can be another source of trouble for unwary executives.

This type of underfunding scenario often occurs when ERP systems are proposed. ERP systems can be hideously expensive—some ERP projects wind up costing $25,000 per user! Here's the rule of thumb: A typical ERP project costs 1 to 2 percent of a company's annual revenue.

Because ERP systems tend to be expensive, they are often sold in modules. The vendor and the CIO agree to "start small," hoping that once the project is underway, more funding will be approved. The project usually begins with HR modules. Then the scope is broadened to include finance modules. Incrementally, the cost of the project escalates until someone in the company notices and begins screaming bloody murder. At this point, the CIO is fired, and another CIO is brought on to "fix the problem."

But the problem isn't the ERP system—the problem is that nobody understood what the ERP system would cost. In a perfect world, the CIO or CFO would meet with the board and say, "The ERP system is going to cost us $25,000 per user—do you still want to go ahead with the project?" At that point, the board would be forced to make a "go/no go" decision.

If they decide not to move ahead, they're stuck with their old systems, but at least they haven't thrown away a lot of money. If they decide to go forward with the project, they know how much it will really cost.

The problem with the incremental approach is that the investment required to get the job done almost always appears much smaller than it actually will be. For one reason or another, the truth of the matter has been obscured.

To my mind, that isn't a good way to conduct business. Nobody wins. The vendor looks bad, the CIO gets fired, and the company is stuck with a system that's only partially built and is not delivering the value that people expected when they agreed to move forward.

Ideally, the new CIO will lay out the true costs of moving forward and completing the project. Then the company can make an informed decision about whether to spend the money and press ahead, or write off the project and begin looking for another solution.

QUESTIONS THE C-SUITE NEEDS TO ASK

1. Are the practical advantages of rebaselining generally understood by the C-suite?

2. Does the C-suite understand the risks and costs associated with shifting funds from existing projects to pay for new projects?

3. Have you explored alternatives to budgeting IT on an annual basis?

CHAPTER 12

The CFO's Perspective

Author's note: Since I thought it would be a good idea to include the perspective of a seasoned finance executive in the book, I turned to Leo Sadovy of SAS, the business software company. Leo is something of a Renaissance man, with a wide range of business experience. At SAS, Leo is currently responsible for world-wide marketing of the company's suite of corporate performance management solutions. Prior to joining SAS, Leo was vice president, finance and business operations, at Fujitsu Ltd. He has an M.B.A. in finance from San Francisco State University.

Instead of merely answering my questions about the various ways in which CFOs typically evaluate IT investments, Leo wrote the following chapter, which I present to you in its entirety.

EXECUTIVE SUMMARY

Every CIO has a contingency fund, but dipping into it too often will be perceived as an indication of poor management. The CFO, the CEO, and the board take capital budgets seriously, and so should the CIO.

Cash, Risk, and Benefits

The starting point for the CFO's evaluation of an IT investment or project would be no different than for any other type of investment. The key issues would be cash, risk, and benefits.

Let's begin with cash. An IT investment will have an impact on the capital budget and on ongoing operational budgets, both in the IT department and elsewhere in the organization.

While the capital budget might initially appear to be just an annual allocation, it is typically always a part of a high-level, multiyear long-range plan, and is further informed by a strategic plan with an even longer horizon. Such investment decisions do not arise overnight, and while a miscellaneous fund for smaller projects is likely included, most significant IT projects would not fall in that category.

Being by nature large cash outlays, they are going to attract a significant level of scrutiny and will require a commensurate level of commitment and management. A two-year, $8 million project needs to be precisely that: $8 million and not a penny more, and not a day longer.

Every CFO worth his/her salt will have a contingency built into the capital budget, but half of that will simply be to cover variability in the available cash flows, with the other half being split among all the projects. If a lackadaisical CIO expects to dip into a 10 percent overrun contingency on each and every IT project, the board will soon find itself engaged in a search for a new CIO.

So the most important rule is: Stay on budget. And on budget usually means on time as well. I know of no eighteen-month IT project that ever stretched to twenty-four months and remained on budget. I'm much less worried about the timing of the cash payments, which can vary considerably from the plan, than I am on hitting each project milestone.

The seriousness with which the CFO, the board, and, by extension, the CIO take the capital budget should not be underestimated. A long-range plan that estimates the availability of operating or financed cash for investment and other purposes is matched against a strategic set of organizational needs and priorities.

In addition to capital investments, other non-internal uses of cash that will be evaluated include dividend payments to shareholders; stock buybacks; refinancing or early payment of debt; taxes due and international cash repatriation; and required increases in working capital (inventory and receivables) as the business grows. Further, other non-capital investments will be considered, such as mergers and acquisitions, market/territory expansion, and new product development.

Strictly within the capital budget, IT will be competing against investment opportunities in plant, property, and equipment across all functions, from warehouses and trucks to a new production line to energy-efficient building improvements.

IT projects are competing against all of these for an organization's scarcest resource: cash. If IT emerges a winner after all that, with the claim of certain benefits after two years and $8 million spent, then by golly it had better deliver on time and on budget as promised, because at $10 or $12 million, the decision could easily have been made to invest that scarce cash elsewhere. The project was made a priority and funded based on a particular business case, and many other projects were left unfunded as lower priorities.

Neither CFOs nor the board like to be tricked into or being held hostage by any project, IT or otherwise, that is going to consume cash that they had better uses for.

Furthermore, often this IT investment is being made in conjunction with other related investments or business reengineering or process improvement initiatives. The benefits depend on all the pieces coming together at the right time. Expansion into a new territory cannot occur without the new CRM system. A new product cannot be launched without a reengineered production process and ERP system. The company cannot capitalize on its new quality initiative if IT development is behind schedule.

Getting more specific regarding IT projects themselves, a CFO would have these sorts of concerns, in roughly this order:

1. *Disruption of ongoing operations* (which could include issues of overall business continuity planning). The worst IT nightmare

is not the two-year, $8 million project that goes five years and $20 million; the worst nightmare is the project that interferes with ongoing operations such that service or delivery commitments cannot be met or that similarly causes significant customer satisfaction issues that harm the brand reputation or corporate image.

2. *Security*. This is not so much about the disclosure of corporate trade secrets as it is about the integrity of the data. Even if I can't get to my stated goal of a three-day close with an earnings release on Day 5, I'd rather be late than *ever* have to restate my numbers because they were accidently or intentionally tampered with. Related to security are my Sarbanes-Oxley (SOX) compliance issues—I can't meet them if there are integrity issues in the IT/data components of the financial processes.

3. *Reporting*. Once I'm satisfied with security, then I do in fact care very much about my commitment to timely reporting, both internally and externally. A commitment to a three-day close with the distribution of the management reporting back on Day 4 means a commitment to meet this goal twelve months out of twelve, not eleven out of twelve. All of the operational supporting systems, not just the financial books, need to be aligned to meet this commitment.

4. *General*: How will the project affect the following general financial/IT concerns:

   a. Upstream—data requirements, existing sources, new data, new calculations, capture, store, transmit, subsystems, and feeder systems

   b. Data warehouse—capacity, data definitions, documentation

   c. Financial processes—allocations, rules, reconciliations, chart of accounts

   d. Downstream—reporting (new or changed), budgets, forecasting, ad-hoc query, taxes, disclosures

We're now finally at a place where we can begin to look at the specifics of the IT value proposition itself, starting with the risks.

- Project sponsorship and leadership
- Composition of the project leadership team and oversight board/process
- Project management (internal and/or external)
- Critical path and built-in money and time contingencies
- Dependencies, internal and external, especially vendors/suppliers
- Milestones
- Impact of delays on related concurrent projects

Project evaluation is an important part of the process. In addition to the numbers and the time lines, what I want from the CIO is an exhaustive evaluation and discussion of the alternatives and options:

- Do nothing
- Use internal development
- Outsource
- Use cloud/SaaS
- Work with partners
- Break work into phases/chunks
- Find alternative approaches to solving the problem and/or achieving the benefit
- Use vendor alternatives: pros and cons
- Use the cheapest vendor? Why or why not?
- Discuss the trade-offs between capital and operating expenses: Should we invest more now to lower future operating costs? Are there less capital-intensive approaches that get us close to the same outcome? ("close" might be good enough; there is no right answer)
- Determine how this approach will affect the cost and complexity of maintenance, support, and migration in the future.

Big picture issues:

- How does this fit with current strategy?
- How does this enable future strategy?
- Where is IT capability going in the future? What new developments are you watching?
- How long can we run on this new platform/project?
- How does this fit in with your IT vision? Your IT architecture for the organization?
- What if we were to invest more now and/or take bigger risks to better prepare for the future?
- What if we delay and wait for the next big thing?
- What can you tell me about support and migration?
- How might this impact other aspects of the business, such as working capital, legal covenants, communications and networking, transparency, and so forth?
- What approaches are our competitors taking to this issue?
- How will this make us more competitive?
- How will this enhance the business processes with which it is associated?
- What about vendor lock-in?
- How can we build on this? What other functions/processes can now take advantage of this new capability?
- How will this project impact things at the personal/cultural/employee level?

IT Project Management:

- What is your project management process (again, as it applies to this project)?
- What IT project metrics will you be watching, and which ones will you be sharing with senior management?
- What significant red flags will you be watching for?

- What's your plan to handle scope creep (internally and externally)? How much contingency do you have to expected scope creep (and don't tell me "none")?
- What's your plan to handle vendors/consultants who expect to recover from a low bid with time and materials (T&M) billings or scope creep?
- Can the vendor/consultant handle it, and if not, what's the contingency plan?
- How does this impact other technical IT issues, like network bandwidth or data storage capacity (I expect these are already in the plan, but I want to make some of them explicit)?
- What can you tell me about knowledge transfer from the vendor/consultant and from the implementation team to the operating team?

The one important issue/viewpoint that I want the board to understand and consider is this: Except in rare cases, there will not be a standalone ROI for this project by itself. IT is much too integrated into our business processes nowadays for that to ever be the case again, like it was in the days when we had standalone "data entry" departments and the like.

In fact, our CIO, if he/she is talented enough, should actually be called our BIO—business information officer. They may have a director of IT working for them whose job it is to understand databases, networks, blade servers, and midtier applications, but the BIO should be focused on how this technology impacts our core business operations and propositions.

How does IT enable our core values, strategy, mission, and vision? This circles back to the opening point about the capital budget: The BIO needs to know how the company's portfolio of IT projects, both ongoing systems and new projects/investments, fits into the overall strategic objectives that eventually drive the final allocation of cash and capital budget in the long-range plan, as well as who understands and supports why *this* project, and not some other, was selected for funding.

As an example, consider the process by which IT projects might be selected for funding in a company that has a newfound focus on quality, with several new quality initiatives across the organization, culminating in a big marketing push that will emphasize quality in next year's messaging and campaigns.

Many factors will have gone into the specifics of the strategic plan, such as what to build versus what to buy, which suppliers to choose, how to monitor both supplier and internal product quality, how to handle returns and repairs and service and customer complaints, production line improvements for better quality, likewise for employee training and education, and so forth.

Information technology could be applied to any and all of these components and functions, but the CIO's evaluation process, working in conjunction with the functional and business unit heads, will lead to perhaps two significant IT investment decisions: monitoring supplier quality and supporting a robust customer contact and communication process. But neither of these alone, or even together, can have an impact or a tangible return on investment (ROI) if the other supplier, production, training, and quality initiatives are not equally successfully implemented.

As the CFO, I don't necessarily need an ROI for any single IT project—this would be very shortsighted on my part. Where I need to start is with the ROI on the larger, strategic business initiative. An overemphasis on specific hard-dollar cost reduction or direct labor and material savings tied directly to a software application or piece of hardware will inevitably lead to poor business decisions.

Soft savings and benefits are fine, but they need strong support, because on the other hand, no CFO is going to be naïve enough to approve funding for an IT project that seems to consist of nothing but ill-defined and loosely connected soft benefits.

I don't require a distinct ROI on my accounting or payroll systems, and neither would I do so for an ERP or CRM system—in the current state of our information age, they are an integral component of the entire enterprise value chain. Even incremental investments are not best judged by their incremental hard benefits, they are best evaluated by their strategic impact on the entire enterprise.

The ROI comes from the overall improvement in the revised business plan that emerges from strategic board discussion around the topic: "What could you do if you had this kind of system/support/process?" This in turn takes buy-in and commitment from the entire management team—success or failure is not all on the back of the CIO.

CHAPTER 13

Optimizing the CEO–CIO Relationship

Author's note: I asked my friend Beverly Lieberman to share her thoughts about the evolving CEO–CIO relationship, and she wrote the following excellent chapter. Beverly is president of Halbrecht Lieberman Associates, Inc., an internationally recognized executive search firm founded in 1957 as Halbrecht Associates. The firm provides retained executive search services across multiple industries while specializing in information technology. Beverly has a B.A. and an M.A. from the University of Michigan and graduated from the prestigious M.I.T. Sloan School Executive Management Program.

EXECUTIVE SUMMARY

To a large extent, the success or failure of a CIO is determined by the quality of his or her working relationship with the CEO and the rest of the C-suite. It's important for CEOs to understand that the tone they set when dealing with the CIO makes a huge difference and can have a significant impact on the success of the company itself.

Making a Strategic Contribution

In our hyperconnected and rapidly evolving digital economy, the quality of the CEO–CIO relationship plays a vital role in the CIO's effectiveness and ultimate success as a strategic contributor.

But there are obstacles to overcome. For example, CIOs have not traditionally reported to CEOs, which means that CEOs have more experience managing other senior executives such as the CFO, the CMO, and the COO. Additionally, CIOs generally rise from the technical ranks as opposed to other parts of management. CIOs tend to live and speak in a complex, jargon-filled world that can be indecipherable to many CEOs and other C-suite executives. As a consequence, it is often difficult for CIOs to make themselves heard and to find acceptance from their peers in the C-suite.

Although the ideal CEO–CIO relationship is based on mutual respect and collaboration, the fact is that most CEOs are more comfortable engaging with their CMOs and CFOs when considering matters of business and strategy, and thus less inclined to turn to their CIOs for advice or input.

Many CEOs tend to view the CIO as someone who operates in a service delivery capacity or in a support function. For years, however, CIOs have been engaged deeply in implementing systems, tools, dashboards, and process improvements that directly enable the CEO's imperatives. That deep engagement creates tremendous opportunities for CEOs to form stronger relationships with their CIOs. From my perspective, CIOs are highly motivated and undervalued strategic resources.

I worked recently with a CEO who asked me to find a CIO who would report directly to him. The CEO told me that he expected technology to play a major role in the company's success going forward, and that he needed a CIO with whom he could have a great working relationship. It turned out that in his previous company, the CIO reported directly to the CEO, and the tight working relationship between the CEO and the CIO had created many benefits and advantages for the company. Guided by his past experience, the CEO had higher expectations about his relationship with the CIO. Based on those higher expectations expressed by the CEO, I found a CIO who could work directly with him.

When I followed up with the CEO, he told me that his new CIO was a great partner and a real asset to the company. Within six months, the new CIO had organized all of the company's key systems in a shared services center, replaced the company's inefficient outsourcing vendors with new efficient vendors, successfully leveraged cloud technology to replace older systems, improved supply chain operations, and dramatically reduced operating costs. It was a great example of how a good working relationship between the CEO and CIO can bring real business benefits to a company.

Clearly this was a case in which the CEO knew that he needed a CIO who understood how technology impacts the business and had the people skills to interact smoothly with the rest of the C-suite.

I believe that those types of working relationships will become more normal and less unusual. When the CEO and the CIO work together, there's a much better chance for the company's resources to be perfectly aligned and sharply focused on solving real business challenges that lead to growth and profitability. At the same time, there are less likely to be the kinds of disconnects and misunderstandings that can delay important IT projects and waste millions of dollars.

That being said, it's not always absolutely critical for the CIO to report directly to the CEO. I recently had a CEO tell me that he simply did not have the time to manage the CIO. Instead, we agreed that the CIO would report to the COO but would also be a member of the CEO's cabinet. As a cabinet member, the CIO would have the visibility and clout necessary to fulfill his responsibilities. My point is that even when the CIO does not report directly to the CEO, there are ways to elevate his or her role in the company and to make certain that IT is viewed as a strategic resource and not merely a support organization.

I recently placed a CIO in a large specialty food company. In addition to his technical skills, the CIO also had expert knowledge of distribution and inventory management. The CEO encouraged the new CIO to spend time in the company's warehouse, where he worked with the head of distribution to improve several key processes that contributed positively to the company's bottom line.

The company wasn't specifically looking for someone with expertise in distribution and inventory management, but that didn't prevent the CIO from making important contributions to the company that went above and beyond traditional IT functions.

Another overlooked area in which CIOs can make major contributions is project management. CIOs are natural project managers, and their experience overseeing expensive long-term capital projects such as ERP implementations is truly unique. Many C-level executives have limited hands-on experience with big capital projects and would probably value the CIO's expertise and experience.

The CIO Evolution

Through experience and education, CIOs are increasingly evolving into business-oriented executives. Many CEOs have discovered that their CIOs are capable of operating as strategic business leaders, much in the same way as their CMOs or CFOs.

CEOs can derive more value from their IT organizations by taking the time to learn basic technology concepts and trends that can impact the success of their company. Technology is a key factor in a company's ability to execute its mission, so it makes perfect sense for the CEO, as well as the entire C-suite, to invest the time required to understand the relationships between technology and the business.

CEOs have a golden opportunity to nurture a valuable competitive resource by setting the right tone for their relationships with CIOs. The best motivational retention tool is to have your CIO play an active, strategic role and do more than execute an endless series of implementations. A CIO who is fully challenged and is able to live up to his/her intellectual potential will not only remain a loyal employee, but will add important value to the company's mission.

Here are some of my professional recommendations for CEOs who want to increase the value of their IT investment by optimizing their relationship with the CIO:

1. Make time for relationship building. The CEO should discuss openly and frequently what is needed in the company

and brainstorm with the CIO to gain assurance that the CIO is in tune with the company's overall strategy. For CEOs who have CIOs reporting to them, a performance review every six months or annually is a perfect opportunity to ask, "What areas would you like to focus on if you weren't busy implementing SAP software?" Many CIOs are eager to contribute their intellectual horsepower to the top line.

2. Encourage the CIO to hire strong lieutenants in order to "keep the trains running" and be freed-up to take on a more active, strategic role.

3. Encourage the CIO to adjust from an IT solution focus to a business strategy focus. Make sure that the CIO has opportunities and forums to spend time with his/her business peers at cross-functional meetings, company-sponsored leadership programs, customer meetings, and team-building initiatives. This can result in a more broad-based CIO who will be better equipped to run IT as a business.

4. Encourage the use of an executive coach for ongoing professional development. Outside coaching gives objective feedback and ample opportunities to enhance relationship building, presentation techniques, and other critical executive management skills.

Companies such as P&G, whose CEO embraces the CIO as a true C-suite partner, have created new competitive advantages that make real differences in their markets. Smart executives know that CIOs have an almost unmatched knowledge of their company's internal operations, business processes, customers' behaviors, and technological capabilities. The CIO's knowledge can and should be channeled into activities that generate tangible benefits for the company. Ideally, the CIO can become an invaluable sounding board and trusted advisor to the CEO and the entire C-suite.

The CEO who invests in his relationship with his CIO and who realizes the value of having a CIO in tune with company strategy will see genuinely valuable results, including new ways of doing business, opportunities to increase efficiency, and truly fresh perspectives on the development of innovative new products and services.

A CEO recently told me that the ideal CIO is a technology rock star who looks like a regular person and speaks in regular business language. The ideal CIO, he said, was a supergeek with excellent people skills. In retrospect, I realized that he was looking for someone who embodies the qualities of both Superman and Clark Kent!

QUESTIONS THE C-SUITE NEEDS TO ASK

1. When you look for a CIO, are you looking for someone to provide services and support, or an executive with the talent and ability to make strategic contributions to the business?

2. Are you encouraging the CIO to learn more about the company's operations and seek experience outside the traditional boundaries of the IT function?

3. Are you actively helping the CIO to become a trusted advisor and key member of the company's C-suite?

CHAPTER 14
Conclusions

EXECUTIVE SUMMARY

Information technology is essential for growth and success in competitive markets. But IT and business strategy must be tightly aligned to avoid wasting time and money. The key to that alignment is good governance and active participation of C-level executives.

As a career IT professional, I am disappointed that Howard Rubin is not more widely known outside the IT industry. In my opinion, Dr. Rubin is the preeminent thought leader of IT economics. His research and his writings provide the best and strongest arguments for investing in IT. In his own words, ". . . technology is a strategic lever, a tool to drive new business growth, protect revenue, reduce business costs and manage risk."

Dr. Rubin has created the Rubin 300, an experimental market index of firms that have been identified as technology leaders. The index, also known as the Technology Leaders Index, or TLI, "tracks the indexed market capitalization of more than 300 leading technology firms in 21 sectors as well as the Dow Jones Industrial Average (DJIA), the Standard & Poor's 500 (S&P 500) and the Fortune 500," writes Dr. Rubin.

The TLI is a truly valuable resource. Smart CIOs will find a wealth of information supporting the critical relationship between IT investment and economic success.

"From January 2006 to Dec. 31, 2010, the TLI has consistently outperformed the S&P 500 and, since the beginning of 2010, has begun to surpass the DJIA. Since the beginning of the study, the TLI has outperformed the S&P 500 by 6.7 percent and the DJIA by 1.2 percent; it has lagged the Fortune 500 by 2.3 percent," writes Dr. Rubin. "These results highlight the importance of strategic technology investment in business performance and imply that technology leaders have overcome the hardships of the economic crisis more quickly than their competitors."[1]

Clearly, Dr. Rubin has established a strong link between IT investment and success in the market. Dr. Rubin makes a great case for investing in IT. As an IT practitioner, I feel indebted to Dr. Rubin for making an objective analysis of the intuitive belief that in our modern economy, technology and profitability are deeply intertwined.

Now let's consider some words of advice from Jim Collins, author of *Good to Great*. In Chapter 7, Technology Accelerators, Collins looks at the connection between technology and commercial success and sees an ambiguous relationship. Some companies seem better at leveraging technology than others, but the reasons are unclear. Collins wonders why top executives at companies that are publicly lauded for their innovative deployment of new technologies rarely mention those technologies as decisive factors in their success.

Collins writes, "If technology is so vitally important, why did the good-to-great executives talk so little about it? Certainly not because they ignored technology; they were technologically sophisticated and vastly superior to their comparisons. Furthermore, a number of the good-to-great companies received extensive media coverage and awards for their pioneering use of technology. Yet the executives hardly talked about technology. It's as if the media articles and the executives were discussing two totally different sets of companies!"

The chapter is instructive because it makes the point that technology by itself is not sufficient for success. The acquisition and deployment of new technology must be linked firmly with clear business objectives. Without that firm linkage, the technology cannot possibly deliver expected value.

Collins sees technology as an accelerator, not as a savior. Perceiving technology as an end unto itself, he suggests, is a trap. Collins puts it succinctly when he writes, "Mediocrity results first and foremost from management failure, not technology failure."

I think that Collins and Dr. Rubin would agree that while technology is critical, it is not a panacea. Wise investment in IT is essential for success, but it is not the only factor in the rise and fall of corporations.

I prefer to speak of technology as an enabler. The word "enabler" suggests that there is already an existing strategy, and that technology's proper role is helping people execute strategy.

The role of enabling strategy is absolutely crucial. Strategic goals are achieved by executing and orchestrating many tasks and processes, some basic and some complex. Since practically every task and process is automated to some degree, IT has become fundamental to execution. That is why it is imperative for IT and company strategy to be aligned as perfectly as possible; if they are not, execution is impossible.

From my vantage point in IT, I see the waste that occurs when IT and company strategy are not tightly aligned. I have come to believe, however, that many of the misalignments I have seen could have been avoided by taking two positive steps:

Step 1. Invest the time and effort required to understand the true nature of IT investments

Step 2. Establish practical and transparent IT governance processes

In most cases, taking those two steps would have made the difference between successful and unsuccessful IT projects.

Step 1 means that the company's C-level executives understand the basics of IT economics, such as the 80/20 rule and the difference between software development and manufacturing.

Step 2 means that the company's C-level executives are committed to and prepared for making informed decisions about IT spending. The best way to prepare for making decisions about IT is by participating in a formal IT governance process. The governance process is the machine that ensures IT investments are aligned with company strategy.

As mentioned earlier, it's important to get away from the idea of IT projects existing in a vacuum. IT projects cannot be detached or separated from business strategy. IT projects exist for the sole purpose of enabling business strategy. The need for IT projects arises from the need to achieve or accomplish specific business goals. As I wrote in Chapter 2, an IT project is not the user interface—it is a collection of underlying processes that, when properly configured, enables the user experience. What you see is the tip of the iceberg, not the project itself.

We undertake IT projects in order to automate or optimize existing business processes, enable new business processes, or transform an ecosystem of business processes. At the most fundamental level, IT projects are business process reengineering projects, nothing more and nothing less. It's really a mistake to call them "IT projects," because that suggests that they are different from "business projects."

In truth, IT projects and business projects are the same thing. The danger of thinking of them as being different is that people tend to apply a different set of rules when considering investments in IT projects. That's a sure recipe for failure. Imagine if you were considering acquiring a business. You would examine every aspect of that business and try your best to determine whether the business was worth buying.

Sadly, that kind of circumspection is rarely applied to purchasing IT systems. Instead, there's a temptation to see IT investments as inherently mysterious and indecipherable. That's a temptation that must be resisted. IT investments can be analyzed and evaluated with the same degree of due diligence that you would apply to any investment decision.

Ignoring risk is almost always a bad idea. Risk doesn't vanish when you ignore it; the more you push it way, the more dangerous it becomes.

Don't Burn Your Money

It's easy to derail an IT project: Just delay it. When you delay an IT project, the costs associated with the project invariably rise. Forget about Moore's Law—cost goes up when you delay an IT project. When cost goes up, ROI goes down. In my experience, delays are a principle cause of IT project failure.

When you delay an IT project, you are quite simply burning the company's money. It's a harsh fact of business that time is money. When you waste time, you waste money. Think of the taxi analogy from Chapter 5. The more you drive around, the more gas you burn. Perhaps an even better analogy would be a jetliner in a holding pattern. The more time the plane spends circling, the more jet fuel it burns. When you consider the cost of jet fuel, it doesn't take long for a profitable flight to become an unprofitable flight.

If concerns about risk are delaying your IT projects, then you should consider setting up "strategic sandboxes" to experiment with new technologies or new approaches to solving problems. I describe the concept of strategic sandboxes in Chapter 6, and I can testify from my own experience that they are a great way to find out what works and what doesn't. They allow you to experiment and innovate without taking huge risks. I recommend them as a prudent way to explore newer technologies that could be turned into competitive advantages.

Strategic sandboxes are also valuable because they force you to confront uncertainty and the possibility of failure. The rapid emergence and adoption of new technologies comes at a price: Lots of those new technologies fail. Despite our best efforts, determining where to place your bets is still more of an art than a science. Early in this book, I quoted Sir Arthur C. Clarke's famous remark that "Any sufficiently advanced technology is indistinguishable from magic." Building on his observation, I think we can say today that the processes involved with developing advanced technology are very similar to the processes involved with creating good art. Both require extraordinary amounts of creativity, and it's exceedingly difficult to put either on a strict timetable.

In Chapter 6, I point out the differences between manufacturing processes and software development processes. Those differences are often overlooked when considering IT projects. Writing software code—and all IT projects require writing new code—is more of an art than a science, and it's certainly not an assembly-line process. Attempts to apply manufacturing practices to software development processes have had mixed success, at best.

Nobody can definitively say, "This software development project will cost $100,000 and will take three months to complete" or "that software development project will cost $250,000 and take six months to complete." Those kinds of projections might be based on someone's experience or on a general rule of thumb, but they will not be accurate projections.

Predicting the cost and length of software development projects is inherently difficult. A better approach would be to present a range of costs over time, with the understanding that there will be an uncertainty factor. The uncertainty factor will be small for smaller projects that can be completed relatively quickly and large for larger projects that stretch out over years.

Large-scale software development projects are a lot like a NASA moon landing. You can try to estimate costs, but your estimates are likely to be wrong because the level of uncertainty increases with the length of the project.

The relationship between uncertainty and time is another argument in favor of completing projects quickly and without delay. The longer you delay a project and the more time it takes to complete, the higher the level of uncertainty will rise.

An effective way of avoiding lengthy projects is by adopting a methodology in which you divide large projects into small pieces and deliver on those small pieces rapidly. Agile methodology was developed for that purpose, and I have found that it can greatly reduce risk and uncertainty in IT projects. If you are not currently using some kind of agile methodology, I recommend that you look into it.

Project management methodology is another area in which the IT department can serve as a guide or trusted advisor to the rest of the enterprise. Members of the IT department generally tend to have deeper experience in project management than their counterparts in other parts of the company.

In its role as the "Office of Know," IT serves as a valuable internal asset with deep project management skills that can be leveraged across many areas of the company. As a CIO, I am very aware of the extent to which IT is involved in practically every aspect of a company's daily processes. The IT department is uniquely positioned to "see across" the company and all of its various units. One of the challenges facing all executives is figuring out how to take advantage of that unique vision.

Again, I think this speaks to the need for a robust governance process that focuses on maintaining the alignment of IT and business strategy. As George Washington knew, there are many strategies and all of them seem great when they are presented. But there can be only one *real* strategy. In Washington's case, the real strategy was winning the war. Nothing else mattered.

Sometimes it seems as though modern companies have many strategies. But each company has one *real* strategy, and IT must be aligned to it in order for the company to succeed and prosper. I think that General Washington would have understood that principle. The Continental Army didn't have an IT department, of course, but it had artillery, which is another kind of technology. As every infantryman knows, the alignment of artillery and infantry is crucial to victory.

In the same way that the American Revolution marked the beginning of a new paradigm for government, the rise of ubiquitous information technology heralds a new paradigm in business. IT will certainly play a key role in this new paradigm. Together, we will face new challenges. As we confront those challenges, let's not lose sight of the opportunities. When IT and business strategy are aligned, we can climb to amazing heights and accomplish great deeds. Let's not be afraid of failure.

Let's calculate the risks honestly, make good decisions based on facts, and move forward bravely.

Note

1. Howard Rubin, "The 'Rubin 300'—An Experimental Market Index of Tech Leaders," *Wall Street & Technology* April 22, 2011: www.wallstreetandtech.com/it-infrastructure/the-rubin-300-an-experimental-market-i/229401005.

RECOMMENDED READING

Barlow, Mike and Michael Minelli. *Partnering with the CIO*. Hoboken, NJ: John Wiley & Sons, 2007.

Brookhiser, Richard. *Founding Father: Rediscovering George Washington*. New York, NY: Free Press Paperbacks, 1997.

— . *George Washington on Leadership*. New York, NY: Basic Books, 2008.

Carr, Nicholas. *The Big Switch: Rewiring the World, from Edison to Google*. New York, NY: W. W. Norton, 2008.

Chambers, Michele, Ambiga Dhiraj, and Michael Minelli. *Big Data, Big Analytics: Emerging Business Intelligence and Analytics Trends for Today's Businesses*. Hoboken, NJ: John Wiley & Sons, 2013.

Christensen, Clayton M. *The Innovator's Dilemma*. New York, NY: Harper Business, 2000.

Christensen, Clayton M. and Michael E. Raynor. *The Innovator's Solution: Creating and Sustaining Successful Growth*. Boston, MA: Harvard Business Review Press, 2003.

Collins, Jim. *Good to Great*. New York, NY: HarperCollins, 2001.

Gladwell, Malcolm. *Outliers: The Story of Success*. New York, NY: Little, Brown and Company, 2008.

Isaacson, Walter. *Steve Jobs*. New York, NY: Simon & Schuster, 2011.

Ishikawa, Kaoru and David J. Lu. *What is Total Quality Control? The Japanese Way*. Upper Saddle River, NJ: Prentice Hall, 1988.

Jones, Daniel T. and James P. Womack. *Lean Thinking: Banish Waste and Create Wealth in Your Corporation*. New York, NY: Simon & Schuster, 1996.

Kahneman, Daniel. *Thinking, Fast and Slow*. New York, NY: Farrar, Straus and Giroux, 2011.

Kotter, John P. *Leading Change.* Boston, MA: Harvard Business School Press, 1996.

Kuhn, Thomas S. *The Structure of Scientific Revolutions (50th Anniversary Edition).* Chicago, IL: University of Chicago Press, 2012.

Liker, Jeffrey. *The Toyota Way: 14 Management Principles from the World's Greatest Manufacturer.* New York, NY: McGraw-Hill, 2003.

Moore, Geoffrey A. *Dealing With Darwin: How Great Companies Innovate at Every Phase of Their Evolution.* New York, NY: Portfolio/Penguin, 2005, 2008.

Rosenstein, Bruce. *Living in More Than One World: How Peter Drucker's Wisdom Can Inspire and Transform Your Life.* San Francisco, CA: Berrett-Koehler, 2009.

ABOUT THE AUTHOR

Greg Fell is currently the chief strategy officer at Crisply, an enterprise SaaS (software-as-a-service) big data company that pioneered the algorithmic quantification of work. Prior to joining Crisply in 2013, Mr. Fell served as vice president and chief information officer of Terex Corporation, where he led a strategic transformation of the IT organization. Terex is a manufacturer of industrial equipment that employs 23,000 persons in fifty manufacturing locations around the globe.

Before joining Terex, Mr. Fell spent nearly twenty years with Ford Motor Company. He started as a developer and worked his way through a variety of management roles supporting the global engineering and manufacturing functions of the company. He has domain expertise on CAD/CAM/CAE systems, lean manufacturing, and control systems.

Mr. Fell is a graduate of Michigan State University and spent several years on staff in the College of Engineering as a senior research programmer and instructor.

Mr. Fell is active in the CIO community and is frequently quoted in books and periodicals for his knowledge of implementing ERP projects and general IT leadership strategies. He is the current president of the Fairfield Westchester Society of Information Managers, a board member with Junior Achievement, and is a mentor of high school students through the First Tee Program.

INDEX